A GUIDE TO COACHING

Resources, Strategies, and Insights for an

Effective Instructional Coaching Program

ISBN-13: 978-0692935170
ISBN-10: 0692935177

For information:
Placer County Office of Education
360 Nevada Street
Auburn CA 95603
530-889-8020

Authored by: Ashley N. Serin

Curriculum and Instruction
Executive Director - Jennifer Hicks

GOLD IN EDUCATION

Gayle Garbolino-Mojica
County Superintendent of Schools

INTRODUCTION

If you are holding this manual, it is because you have made the decision to embark upon an instructional coaching journey. You may be an administrator seeking to understand the role of a coach and the ways a coach can benefit teachers, your site, and your district. Or you may be an instructional coach looking for skills, strategies, tips, and tricks to maximize your effectiveness. Perhaps, you are somewhere in the middle. Either way, this guide has been written for you.

The following pages are not designed to be read through from cover to cover. Instead, this guide is designed as a resource. Simply flip to the topic of interest and begin reading. This coaching guide covers everything from starting a coaching program, to staying organized, and much more.

As you read through this guide, be aware that the terms *instructional coach, IC, TOSA, and Teacher on Assignment* all refer to the same position.

The creation of this guide came from instructional coaches within Placer County. Much of this material was envisioned from our county-wide coaching PLC meetings, formal interviews of ICs at each district, and continual review from site leaders, district administrators, and coaches. It is not simply one person's creation, but rather a collaboration of what instructional coaching looks like in action on a daily basis.

Our vision at the Placer County Office of Education is to provide exemplary leadership and service to schools, parents, and the community as we work together to provide a globally competitive, comprehensive, rigorous and relevant education for all students. This guide is one of the many ways we are supporting you and your educational impact in these golden foothills.

So, grab your cup of coffee and your growth mindset, and let's dive in.

NOTES FOR DIGITAL READERS

- For ease of use, this document has been linked throughout. Any underlined word or phrase, when clicked, will either take you directly to a page within the document or to an external source.

- The Table of Contents is linked and will take you directly to the page of your choice.

- To return to the Table of Contents at any time, click on *A GUIDE TO COACHING* found at the bottom of every page.

TABLE OF CONTENTS

WHAT IS INSTRUCTIONAL COACHING?

INSTRUCTIONAL COACHING DEFINED

Instructional Coaching, as defined by Jim Knight, is a *partnership approach to improving instruction*. Instructional coaches come alongside teachers as professional collaborators, helping them incorporate research-based instructional practices into their classroom, and following-up with them on current initiatives and new learning. Coaches must be trained and confident in effective communication, with a strong capacity to empathize, listen, build trusting relationships, and pose questions for impact. A strong component of an instructional coach is the ability to utilize reflective practices that hit deep into the client to ignite change. But coaching is more than the one-on-one partnership described above. Instructional coaches are the boots on the ground of professional development, from surveying teachers and administrators in an effort to determine areas of need, to providing specific training, workshops, and seminars, to facilitating PLCs and other team meetings, and finally following up with teams and individuals in the implementation of the new practice, curriculum, or initiative. Instructional coaches dance through their professional relationships with administrators and teachers, acting as neither, yet supporting both. Refer to Defining Your Role (p. 43) for additional descriptions and elevator speeches of instructional coaching.

> "There are two ways of spreading light; to be the candle or the mirror that reflects it."
>
> -Edith Wharton-

REFLECT

* How have you previously defined instructional coaching?
* Based on this description, what do you need to adjust to ensure that your IC program is in alignment with the purpose of instructional coaching?
* What would you add to this definition to fully demonstrate the work of an instructional coach?

FROM THE FIELD

When I entered into my first position as an instructional coach, I didn't really know exactly what that meant. As I worked with other coaches and TOSAs throughout that year, I realized that I wasn't the only one. Not only was the definition of an IC unknown to me and my colleagues, but many administrators and teachers didn't fully understand the role either. It wasn't until I analyzed my job description, read a ton of books on coaching, and got into the field that I was finally able to wrap my mind around the purpose, goals, and duties of an IC. My hope is that the research I have done and presented in this guide will help you as you begin to understand the power of instructional coaching.

COACHING AS PROFESSIONAL DEVELOPMENT

"The purpose of staff development is not just to implement instructional innovations; its central purpose it to build strong collaborative work cultures that will develop the long-term capacity for change."
-Michael Fullan-

Research has proven that the traditional means of professional development, the one and done style of training, has very little impact on classroom practice. Joyce and Showers proved that the transfer of knowledge and skill learned in a training increases from 5% to 95% with coaching. If our goal is to impact student learning in the classroom, and shift teacher practice, then we must increase the transfer rates of our teachers. With coaching, this is possible.

Components	Knowledge	Skills	Transfer
Study of Theory	10%	5%	0%
Demonstration	30%	20%	0%
Practice	60%	60%	5%
Peer Coaching	95%	95%	95%

Based on Joyce and Showers Research (2002)

The effectiveness of professional development is dependent upon the support and follow-up provided to a teacher after the training has occurred. Utilizing a coach helps teachers transfer their training to the classroom in the following ways:

- ✓ Practicing new strategies more frequently and developing greater skill
- ✓ Using strategies more appropriately
- ✓ Increasing long term retention of the knowledge and skill of the strategies
- ✓ Being more likely to explain new models of teaching to students, ensuring students understand the purpose and expected behaviors
- ✓ Exhibiting clearer cognition with regard to the purpose and use of the strategies

Additional findings from the *Annenberg Foundation for Education Reform* state that effective coaching:

- ✓ Encourages collaborative, reflective practice
- ✓ Allows teachers to apply their learning more deeply, frequently, and consistently than teachers working alone
- ✓ Affects the culture of a school or system in a positive way
- ✓ Increases teachers' use of data to inform practice
- ✓ Supports collective leadership across a school system

Reflect

❖ Based on the *Joyce and Showers* and *Annenberg Foundation* research, how can you best use instructional coaches in your school or district?

❖ Which of the findings listed above stand out to you the most? How can you take this understanding and apply it to your role?

❖ Think about a time when you learned something new. What made the greatest impact on your learning?

FROM THE FIELD

Anyone who has played sports understands the power of a coach. The power of having someone in the field with you, standing right on the side of the court, guiding you, encouraging you, and shaping you while you are in the middle of the action. And while I played sports in high school, one of my most powerful coaching experiences came from the other side of the social ladder - musical theater. It was two weeks until opening day and I was the lead role in Bye Bye Birdie. I had one scene in particular where my character, Rosie Alvarez, was supposed to be enraged, furious, calling it quits and walking out on the love of her life. As a 15 year old girl with a pretty wonderful childhood, I didn't know where to pull this anger from, so my director brought in an acting coach. My high school won awards for their drama program, so this level of commitment was pretty standard. The coach worked with me three times during those last two weeks, and the first two times we never even walked onstage. We sat and talked. He guided me to connect with the character, focus on the emotion, and find what mattered. He discussed the stage set up and props and asked me how my character could manipulate those props to portray the intense frustration of the scene. He didn't tell me what to do, but instead guided me to find my best way of portraying this character in this particular scene. The final session we were on stage, just the two of us, running through the scene. He was right next to me, pointing out subtleties and reminding me of what we had discussed earlier, pulling out that emotion as I walked the steps of the scene. After I ran the scene in front of the producer and the director, the feedback I received was powerful. The director was amazed, excited, and proud of what the scene had become. Years later, the director and I would talk about that one scene, and how I had never acted better in my entire life than I did in the five minutes I was alone onstage in Bye Bye Birdie as a 15 year old girl. This reality has rung true for me throughout the years. For as I reflect on the moments when I have learned the most, there is always someone by my side walking me through the process and working with me to achieve my goals. Instructional coaches are the acting coaches of education!

COACHING IMPACT AND SUPPORT OF STATE AND FEDERAL INITIATIVES

The focus of all educators is increased student learning through a high quality education. In order to provide this high quality education, teachers must have high quality teaching practices and strategies. Coaching supports teacher practices by ensuring strong implementation of learning initiatives, maximizing the use of adopted curriculum, and ultimately inciting change and growth in the classroom.

According to Malcolm Gladwell, the author of *Outliers: The Story of Success,* mastering a complex skill, such as teaching, requires 10 thousand hours of deliberate practice. That equates to 7 years for teachers working in schools. Coaching allows for increased deliberate practice time for the teacher and creates positive change and teaching mastery in less time. Refer to Measuring the Impact of Coaching (p. 51) for more information on data collection, feedback surveys, and evidence used in determining impact.

Between the Local Control Accountability Plan (LCAP), Multi-Tiered Systems of Support (MTSS), and Common Core State Standards (CCSS), district and site leaders are seeking ways to meet all priorities and serve their students effectively. Instructional coaching supports these processes.

> Coaching supports teacher practices by ensuring strong implementation of learning initiatives, maximizing the use of adopted curriculum, and ultimately inciting change and growth in the classroom.

Local Control Accountability Plan (LCAP)

The LCAP requires district offices to prove they are meeting the following 8 priorities:

1. Basic Services
2. Implementation of Common Core State Standards
3. Parental Involvement
4. Student Achievement
5. Student Engagement
6. School Climate
7. Course Access
8. Other Student Outcomes

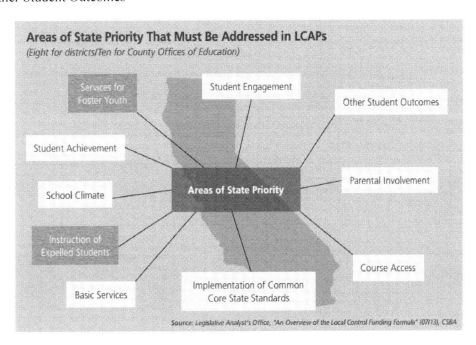

Coaching supports these priorities in the following ways:

➢ Basic Services: Ensuring all teachers are qualified and up-to-date on current best practices and classroom strategies, and supporting teachers in the implementation of newly adopted and aligned curriculum.
➢ Implementation of Common Core State Standards: Providing teachers with professional development, training, follow-up, implementation, and more for the successful utilization of Common Core in the classroom.
➢ Student Achievement: Increasing student assessment data through implementation of proven methods of teaching and support of teachers in the process; increasing the analysis of data among teachers through training, modeling, and collaboration.
➢ Student Engagement: Working with teachers to design motivating and engaging lessons that reach all learners.
➢ School Climate: Working with teachers and leaders to create a collaborative community, geared toward student learning, and positive change.
➢ Other Student Outcomes: Supporting teachers in ensuring access to all student groups, supporting all student populations, and utilizing a variety of assessment strategies to gauge learning.

Multi-Tiered Systems of Support (MTSS)

California's MTSS requirements ensure all students have access to and achieve high quality levels of learning. The four core components of MTSS, according to the California Department of Education, are:

1. *High-quality, differentiated classroom instruction.* All students receive high-quality, standards-based, culturally and linguistically relevant instruction in their general education classroom settings by highly qualified teachers, who have high academic and behavioral expectations, attained through differentiated learning instructional strategies, such as Universal Design for Learning.

2. *Systemic and sustainable change.* MTSS principles promote continuous improvement processes at all levels of the system (district, school site, and grade/course levels). This is accomplished through collaborative restructuring efforts, identifying key initiatives, collecting, analyzing, reviewing data, and implementing supports and strategies based on data that are then refined as necessary to sustain effective processes.

3. *Integrated data system.* District and site staff collaborate to create an integrated data collection system that includes assessments such as state tests, universal screening, diagnostics, progress monitoring, and teacher observations at the site to inform decisions about tiered support placement, as well as data collection methods such as parent surveys for continuous systemic improvement.

4. *Positive behavioral support.* District and school staff collaboratively select and implement schoolwide, classroom, and research-based positive behavioral supports for achieving important social and learning outcomes. A strong focus on integrating instructional and intervention strategies supports systemic changes based on strong, predictable, and consistent classroom management structures across the entire system.

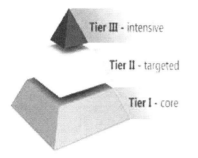

MTSS pushes for strong first-instruction that meets the needs of all learners; a component that is specifically supported by instructional coaches. Through professional development, training, follow-up, demo lessons, and more, instructional coaches work with teachers to implement research-based first instruction strategies and methods in their classrooms.

REFLECT
- ❖ As you review the LCAP priorities and MTSS components, which elements do you see are most positively influenced by instructional coaches?
- ❖ How can you keep these goals at the forefront of your work in the field of instructional coaching?

FROM THE FIELD

Throughout conversations I've had this year with administrators and coaches, I've seen a trend in the topic of coaching relevance and the ways instructional coaching fits into the accountability and support systems of education today. It's an interesting conversation because anyone involved in the coaching program, from administrators to ICs to teachers, can easily see the impact and value of the program. Those outside of the IC program, however, tend to wonder about the connection of coaching to current state initiatives. And unfortunately, when faced with a budget crisis, the first positions to go are the coaches. But, this should not be the case. The data and the support coaches offer to LCAP priorities and MTSS components proves the effectiveness of these coaching programs. I fully believe that every district should have a coaching program built into their LCAP and MTSS plans because coaches are the only way to get a 95% transfer rate of new learning into the classroom. That's ultimately what this is all about, right? It's about increasing access to high levels of learning for all students. The only way to do so is to impact teacher practice within the classroom. Coaches are the ones who do that. I'm passionate about this work of instructional coaching and I know that the information included in this guide will provide the support and data needed to keep ICs in districts!

ROLES OF A COACH

Instructional Coaches take on more roles that what can simply be defined by the term 'coach'. Within that title are multiple roles that support teachers and administrators within the school system.

Professional Developer

Instructional coaches provide professional development, training, and ongoing learning to teachers and school sites in the areas of site goals and district specific initiatives. They facilitate and run PD sessions, site-wide and district-wide professional development days, as well as provide one-on-one or team PD through coaching cycles. ICs are responsible for the professional development roll-out, follow-up, and extension work. They work to design and implement job-embedded PD that is collaborative, standards focused, and effective. ICs collect data on the PD wants and needs of the teachers, design their PD to meet those needs, and follow up with teachers on implementation of their learning. Refer to Professional Development (p. 48) for information on how to run an effective PD session.

Instruction Specialist

ICs provide and support the implementation of effective instructional strategies and pedagogy for presenting content and increasing student learning. An ICs job is to attend trainings and read resources to learn new best practices, and then support teachers in implementing those practices. Strong instruction spans across all grade levels and subject areas, which is why this specific role is one of the most popular for an instructional coach.

Curriculum Specialist

Instructional coaches make selections, facilitate pilots, support adoptions, provide training, and coach teachers and teams in the implementation of new curriculum and programs. They work with teachers and teams to ensure curriculum is aligned to standards and accessible to all students, and to ensure the curriculum within the class is used appropriately and with fidelity.

Standards and Frameworks Expert

Instructional coaches collaboratively work with teachers and teams to break down the standards, utilize the framework, align curriculum to the standards, create pacing guides, determine scope and sequence, and identify changes and shifts in the content. They attend specific meetings and trainings on the standards and the frameworks in support of this work.

Intervention Specialist

ICs work with teachers and teams on best meeting the needs of students through effective first instruction, adapting new curriculum to allow access for all learners, and supporting teachers with intervention strategies and resources. ICs work with teachers and teams on differentiation and universally designed lessons. They train and coach educators on meeting the needs of all students using system wide and class wide intervention supports.

Data Coach

ICs ensure that student data is used to drive instruction, programs, curriculum, and student learning. They support teachers and teams in utilizing assessment programs and analyzing data to inform instruction. ICs understand the 3 rules of data as outlined by Tom Many in *Leverage*: "(1) easily accessible and timely, (2) purposefully arranged, and (3) publicly discussed." ICs provide teams with Data Analysis Protocols such as Here's What, So What, Now What and others, which can be found in the Appendix.

Resource Provider

ICs work with teachers and teams to research and gather a variety of resources that support student learning, teacher practice, instruction, curriculum, intervention, and more. They then work with teachers and teams to ensure that the resources are utilized properly for maximum impact.

Equity Supporter

ICs work with teachers and teams to ensure equity and access to all students in the classroom. They provide articles and research on culturally responsive teaching, support and training on solid first instruction, Universal Design for Learning and more. ICs review data with teachers to point out disproportionality and ensure intentionality in the inclusion of all students.

Team Facilitator

ICs facilitate and run professional learning community (PLC) teams, as well as other collaborative team meetings. They use the components of a PLC (focus on learning, collaborative culture, results-oriented), with protocols, as they work with teams in maximizing their time together. They form and maintain site wide and district wide teams to work toward initiative implementation. Refer to Professional Development (p. 48) for more information on the use of protocols.

Capacity Builder

ICs understand their role to build capacity in teachers and teams, who will then continue in their new learning even after the coaches have left. ICs coach, facilitate, train, provide space, model, co-teach, plan, prepare, collaborate, and work alongside teachers in an effort to build in them the capacity, skills, and ability to reach all students and grow as an educator.

Additional Coaching Roles

Some sites and districts hire Instructional Coaches under a different name, such as a Teacher on Special Assignment (TOSA) or a Teacher on Assignment (TOA). Many districts and sites also have content specific positions such as an English Language Arts (ELA) Coach, a Technology Coach, a Science Coach, and more. In these cases, the coach (or TOSA) will focus on the content of their position while continuing to build capacity, provide professional development, adopt curriculum, incorporate instructional strategies, etc.

REFLECT

❖ Which of the roles of an instructional coach is your strength, and which is an area of growth for you? What can you do to improve in all of these coaching roles?

❖ Set up a meeting with the coach and the supervisor to review these coaching roles. Determine which ones will be your focus, and how much of your time will be spent in each role.

FROM THE FIELD

One of the most difficult parts for me when I began as an instructional coach was the lack of knowledge surrounding what exactly I was supposed to do. What I've learned, however, is that instructional coaching covers a wide range of roles and responsibilities. By knowing ahead of time what is expected of me as a coach, I can spend less time trying to decipher why I'm here, and more time diving into these roles and making a positive impact. I also learned the value in knowing what my roles are so I can know which projects to accept with open arms, and which ones to push back on as they are not appropriate to my position. My first month as an instructional coach, I realized that I was not being utilized in the position I was hired for. One teacher in particular was asking me to make copies and create worksheets, and an administrator I worked with was asking me to train the teachers on logging onto and maneuvering through the new Learning Management System. Neither of these were within my scope as an instructional coach, but because I didn't know that yet, I accepted these tasks. It took up valuable time from my coaching cycles and my ability to professionally develop teachers, and it put a false understanding in the minds of the staff of what exactly I was there to do. I had to then work hard to undo the mindset that my purpose is simply to do for the staff what they don't want to do themselves. However, once I learned exactly what my role entailed, I was able to politely decline certain project requests and state with confidence the roles for which I am responsible, which has led to a greater understanding of instructional coaching among all stakeholders, and greater impact in my work at the district.

COACHING TEAMS

"Professional Learning Communities have emerged as arguably the best, most agreed-upon means to improve instruction and student performance." - M.J. Schmoker

The work of an instructional coach extends beyond the individual one-on-ones with a teacher. Instead, the coach's impact covers PLCs and teams as well. Throughout the region, coaches are utilized in the team setting, rather than the individual setting, with more and more districts moving to this team coaching model. As a coach of a team, the ICs role changes slightly. You must now be skilled in effectively facilitating and running a PLC or a Collaborative Team. Protocols become imperative to ensure the time is maximized and valued among team members.

> "The most valuable resource that all teachers have is each other. Without collaboration, our growth is limited to our own perspective."
> -Robert John Meehan-

The three big ideas of a PLC are (1) A Focus on Learning, (2) A Collaborative Culture and (3) A Results Orientation. Whether you are in a grade-alike or subject-alike team having the ability to create common assessments, or you are part of an interdisciplinary or multi-grade level team, these three big ideas should still be utilized. Instructional coaches working with teams are responsible to facilitate the actions around these three ideas and provide teams with protocols and practice in becoming self-sustaining PLCs. Coaches can still follow a coaching cycle with teams as outlined in The Coaching Cycle (p. 34), or they can facilitate lesson studies. Most team coaching will follow specific topics as outlined below.

Type of Team	Members	Topics
Professional Learning Community	Grade-alike or subject-alike	○ Creating a scope and sequence ○ Curriculum development and Implementation ○ Lesson Design ○ Common Assessments ○ Data analysis
Collaborative Team	Multiple grade levels, interdisciplinary	○ Instructional Strategies ○ Intervention Strategies ○ Literacy Standards ○ School-Wide Initiatives such as Universal Design for Learning

As the coach of the PLC or the Collaborative Team, your job is make sure the group is functioning under the three strands of an effective PLC. Tom Many clearly outlines the role of coaching teams in his book, *Amplify your Impact: Coaching Collaborative Teams in PLCs at Work*.

First, teams must have a focus on learning. It is not about teaching, but about learning. Team members must constantly ask themselves what the students are learning, and how they can support students in their learning. A focus on learning includes a guaranteed and viable curriculum, strong instructional strategies, and more. When the conversation is on what the students have learned, and not on what the teacher has taught, then real change can begin to happen.

Second, the team must have a collaborative culture, which includes transparency, a mindset of openness, respect, trust, the sharing of ideas, and an agreement to the norms of collaboration. Refer to the Seven Norms of Collaboration (p. 26) to begin this collaborative culture.

The final component of a PLC model is a results orientation. The team remains focused on data and evidence of student learning at high levels, analyzing the data, determining effectiveness, making changes, analyzing the data again, etc. Many teams use the Plan - Study - Do - Act Model as a results orientation, as well as other Data Protocols. Refer to the Appendix for samples. It is not about what feels good, or looks good, but about what is ultimately effective in ensuring students are learning at high levels.

As the coach of the team, you are responsible to ensure the work of a PLC is happening by utilizing protocols to build a system of change among the team, ensuring norms are maintained, and guiding the team into a focus on learning, a collaborative culture, and a results orientation. Refer to the Appendix for a sample PLC Agenda and Template.

REFLECT

- ❖ What are the expectations for coaching teams within your instructional coaching program?
- ❖ How familiar are you with the PLC model?
- ❖ What questions do you still have regarding the PLC process, and who can you go to for support in answering those questions?

FROM THE FIELD

When I started in a position as instructional coaching specialist, I was given the responsibility of facilitating monthly PLC meetings which were optional for coaches throughout the county. The only problem was that I did not have any experience in running a PLC; I had only ever been a part of one. So my first few meetings were essentially me asking the team if they had anything they wanted to discuss. Yep. Great work. I know. Needless to say, the meetings began to fall apart. Less and less people would show up because they didn't see the value, or they wouldn't get a chance to share because one person would take up the whole conversation. I needed to make a change and make it fast. Thankfully, I attended a Tom Many training on PLCs and protocols which completely changed the way I saw team meetings. So, in March of that year (yes, it took me THAT long to figure this out), I created a Google Doc Template and put in place norms, a vision, a structure, and a protocol to our meetings. Now in our meetings, we all log into the shared doc. We review the norms and vision of the team, and the agreed upon strategy and focus from last month. Then we take 5 minutes to type our experiences with the strategy, data and evidence from the strategy, links to any important information, etc. After that time, we start with the first one typed onto the document and ask for the member to explain. Each member gets 3 or so minutes to explain their work, experience, and data with the strategy. The team learns from each member, gets resources through the linked documents, and every voice is able to be heard around the table. Not only did our attendance double in just the two months until the end of that year, but the perceived value of the PLC skyrocketed. It's apparent that the use of a protocol can completely transform a meeting.

THE BLENDED COACHING MODEL

> "Coaching is a complex art, and we are convinced there is not a single 'right' way to approach it."
> -Gary Bloom-

In the same way teachers understand that every student learns differently, so too, coaches must understand that every teacher learns differently. Depending on the topic, the purpose, the client, and the goal, a coach should travel between a variety of coaching styles and models. For example, if a coach tries to address a new teacher's plea for advice by asking reflective questions through cognitive coaching, she is doing that teacher a disservice. On the other hand, if a coach wears his consultant hat with the 25 year veteran of the English department, he will most likely negatively affect his rapport within that relationship. Different coaching models are required for different scenarios throughout instructional coaching.

Outlined below are 6 coaching models of which all coaches should be both familiar and comfortable.

Cognitive Coaching
Cognitive coaching is a non-judgmental process that encourages and supports individuals as they move beyond their present capacities into new behaviors and skills. Cognitive coaches support their clients in becoming more resourceful, informed and skillful. They attend to the internal thought processes and do not work to change overt behaviors. In the cognitive coaching model, the coach does not need to be an expert on the topic, but instead an expert in communication and reflection techniques. They seek to change the deeper seated issues rather than the external actions of the client.

Facilitative Coaching
Facilitative coaching builds on the client's existing skills, knowledge, interpretations and beliefs and helps the client construct new skills, knowledge, interpretations and beliefs. A facilitative coach does not focus on sharing professional expert knowledge, but rather supports the client in developing the capacity to build expertise through self-actualized, reflective practice. The locus of control in facilitative coaching leans towards the client. Similarly, in facilitative coaching, the coach helps the client gather and interpret data and feedback, develop his or her own interpretations, and analyze and select courses of action.

Collaborative Coaching
The collaborative coach helps the client prioritize and develop a plan. In collaborative coaching it is understood that both the client and the coach have a significant amount of knowledge and will accomplish the most when working in conjunction with one another. A collaborative coach gets her hands dirty and does at least some portion of the work alongside the client. The focus is on concrete action with a larger goal to develop knowledge, skills, and internal capacity that can be generalized to other situations. This model of coaching is appropriate when the coach and client have identified a need or problem conducive to shared work that promises to generate powerful learning for the client. One important principle to remember is that collaborative coaching is not about the coach rescuing an overwhelmed client.

Instructional Coaching
A purely instructional coaching style is one that is direct in approach. The instructional coach shares his or her own experience, expertise, and craft wisdom with the client by using traditional teaching strategies, which may include modeling, providing resources and direct instruction. The coach may provide the client with something the client lacks, and is often used when direct action is required on a rather timely basis.

Consultative Coaching

Another way to explain consultative coaching is the traditional mentoring style. This style of coaching relies on the specific expertise a coach can bring to a coaching relationship. The coach in this setting has some influence over the client, but no direct power or authority to make changes. The consultative coach shares perspective, knowledge and advice, but does not own or participate in any action that results from the coaching process. He or she focuses on specific things, usually technical in nature, and might carry out data gathering for the client or even provide specific recommendations in particular situations.

Transformational Coaching

Transformational coaching is a deeper level of coaching that helps the client change and develop who they are as a professional. It is based on the belief that people are capable of making fundamental, internal changes. Strong transformational coaching influences personality, disposition and interpersonal skills, while moving people beyond improved performance, to developing new ways of thinking, and ultimately changing their way of being.

The important element to remember is that a strong coach is one who is able to move swiftly between the styles and models as needed throughout a coaching relationship. For example, if a coach is trained in the newly adopted curriculum and directed to provide training, support, and coaching to the 3rd grade team on that curriculum, then she will wear a consultative hat. However, as the team begins to implement the training and meet with the coach one-on-one to discuss their process in working with the new curriculum, the coach may move into more of a facilitative role. Sometimes the coach will need to jump in with the teacher in collaborative planning, or offer a demo lesson of the curriculum in an instructional coaching style. It is the mark of a strong coach to know which model is needed in which scenario to maximize the growth and learning of the teacher.

REFLECT

❖ Which coaching model is your area of strength, and which is an area of growth for you?

❖ Think about a recent coach meeting you've had with a client. Which coaching model did you adopt in this meeting? Why?

❖ How can an understanding of these different models benefit you as a coach?

FROM THE FIELD

Before I knew what instructional coaching truly entailed, I was afraid that I had to be an expert who went in and shared all of my knowledge with the teachers with whom I was working. This belief brought me a ton of anxiety and stress on many levels. Then I learned that consultative coaching is only one piece of the pie. Thank goodness. I find that I am most comfortable with collaborative coaching and instructional coaching and that those models fit best with the program in which I am currently involved. Sometimes, though, when I meet with a teacher, I'll realize that the collaborative planning and instructional demo lessons need to be put on hold, so I can provide reflection through facilitative coaching on an issue the teacher is dealing with in the moment. These models felt uncomfortable to me at first, but after experience with them, I am now able to determine within the first few minutes of the conversation, which style I will need to utilize. With that being said, I still must continue working on improving my skills in specific styles! I know I will continue to grow in these models, as I focus on meeting the teacher where they are and using my coaching skills to help them move toward their goals.

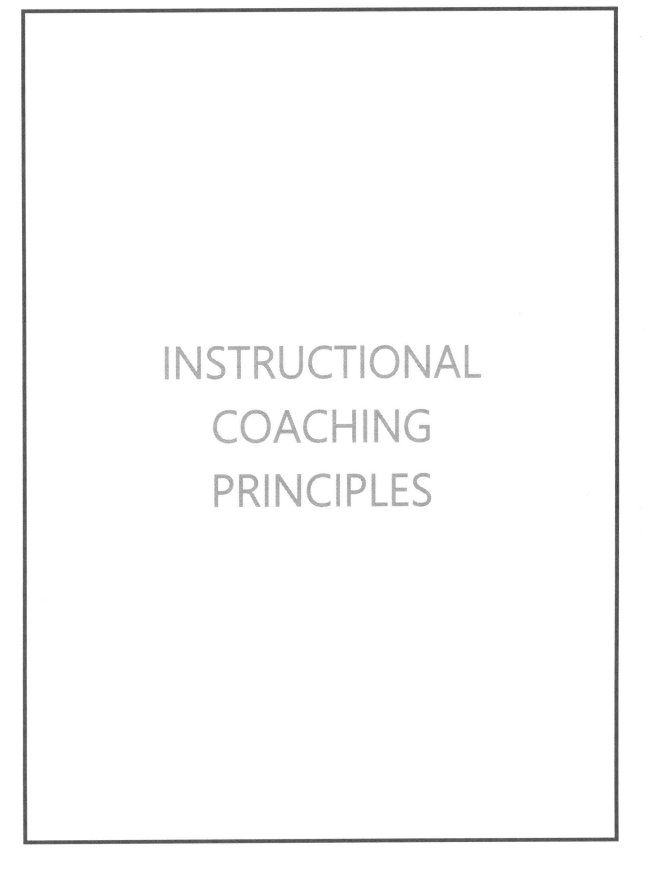

INSTRUCTIONAL COACHING PRINCIPLES

IT'S ALL ABOUT RELATIONSHIPS

Before any effective coaching can take place, the coach must understand that her work is based entirely on her ability to form a strong professional relationship with her clients. Such relationship forming falls under two categories: a coaching mindset and trust.

> "You have to build a relationship before you can do anything. You have to truly care about the individuals you are working with."
> -Lynn Barnes-

Coaching Mindset

According to *Leadership Coaching for Educators*, the ability to achieve long-term success requires coaches to develop an attitude and philosophy toward people that views them in a positive light and as continuous learners. The relationship coaches develop with their clients depends greatly on how they see them, which requires coaches to adopt particular characteristics. A strong coach must be:

➢ An Active Listener
➢ Nonjudgmental
➢ A Possibility Thinker
➢ Compassionate
➢ Inspirational
➢ Personable
➢ Intuitive
➢ Sincere

➢ Trustworthy
➢ A Risk-Taker
➢ Action-Oriented
➢ Focused on Results
➢ Knowledgeable in Core Coaching Competencies
➢ Curious

As you embark upon this coaching journey, assess yourself based on these characteristics. Determine which come naturally, and which will need to be practiced and intentional for you. The ability to master these mindsets will determine your success as a coach.

Trust

Since relationships are at the heart of coaching, a strong coach knows how to build, maintain, and fully utilize trust in the coaching relationship.

"The role of a coach is granted by the coachee based on trust. Without trust there can be no coaching. Trust will always be at stake during the process of coaching. The trust can increase and become more solid, and it can be taken away. It can be initially gained, then lost for good. One of the big mistakes a coach can make is always moving along the thin cord of the coachee's trust." - *Mastering the Art of Professional Coaching*

Thankfully there are tried and true ways to establish and maintain trust with a client. Below are 10 steps to building trust with a client.

1. Cautiously gather background information: While you might be tempted, do not let other people's perceptions shape your thinking.

2. Establish confidentiality: Make this an explicit and publicly discussed norm with your client. Come back to it multiple times to reiterate the power of confidentiality, and, of course, stay confidential.

3. Listen: Listening is one of the most powerful components of coaching. Strong listening builds trust, establishes rapport, guides practice, uncovers beliefs, changes thoughts, implements actions and more. Refer to Listening (p. 23) for more information.

4. Ask questions: Seek to truly understand and authentically show interest by asking questions that are directly related to your listening. Trust is built when a client believes that their coach actually cares. Listening to what they are saying, and then asking questions regarding their thoughts, or inquiring for more information is one way to encourage this.

5. Connect: As Maya Angelou says, "I note the obvious difference between each sort and type, but we are more alike, my friends, than we are unalike." We must find common ground with our clients. How do we do this? Hold conversations with your clients around the following topics: interests, convictions, activities, roles, and experiences. If you listen deep enough you will find commonality in at least one area. Once you do, verbalize that commonality and check in with them often regarding it. Making these personal connections builds trust with our clients.

6. Validate: People want to feel respected and heard. Be intentional about validating the strengths, assets, and experiences of your client. Be authentic in your validation. Refer to Presuming Positive Intent (p. 27) for more information.

7. Be open: Trust begins with you. Be open about who you are and what you do. Discuss why you do what you do, and your passions and beliefs in this position, while always being honest.

8. Ask for permission to coach: Even if you are in a position that mandates coaching for teachers, it is still important to ask for their permission. Discuss that you are here to collaborate together; define your role, and the coaching expectations; share about yourself; then, ask if they are open and willing to go along this journey with you. This little statement at the end of your initial meeting will work wonders with your client. Also, throughout the coaching relationship, be sure to ask for permission in other areas. Statements, formed as permissions, will provide your client with autonomy, a strong need in adult communication. Refer to Andragogy (p. 31) for more information.

9. Keep commitments: If you say you will do it; do it.

10. Plan and prepare: Keep track of your coaching conversations through Coaching Logs, reflective journals, and other protocols. Prepare for the meeting before entering and be sure to plan well for future meetings. Refer to the Coaching Cycle (p. 34) for more information.

As you work on relationship building with your clients, keep this information in mind, and remember that building trust takes times.

REFLECT

❖ Review the list of characteristics for a coaching mindset. Which ones are strengths, and which are areas of growth? How can you begin to improve in all of these areas?

❖ How do you gain and maintain trust? Review these steps and pick 3 to focus on within your role this year.

FROM THE FIELD

I used to think trust came naturally to me. Everyone trusts me. I'm a trustworthy person. Oh, how I was wrong. It is very different to go from a classroom teacher to a coach who works one-on-one with teachers, sits at the table with administrators, and facilitates PLCs. I quickly realized that some teachers did not trust me, not because of anything I had done, but because of their past experiences, or their lack of trust in the system as a whole, or their fear of anyone who appears to be in an authoritative position, even though I wasn't. I even had one teacher directly tell me all of this. Unfortunately, I was entering these relationships with a bad reputation before they even knew my name! I discovered that slowly through the steps outlined above, my constant positivity, and my willingness to listen, respect, and be transparent, I began to break through those issues, and gain trust as a colleague and a professional. For some, it takes time, but the good news is that the seemingly abstract quality of trust can actually be made very tangible through the steps outlined above.

LISTENING

"Listening is only powerful and effective if it is authentic. Authenticity means that you are listening because you are curious and you care, not just because you are supposed to." – D. Stone

"When you talk, you are only repeating what you already know; but if you listen, you may learn something new."
-Mahatma Ghandi-

"If we try to listen we find it extraordinarily difficult, because we are always projecting our opinions and ideas, our prejudices, our background, our inclinations, our impulses; when they dominate, we hardly listen at all to what is being said." - William Isaacs

One of the key instructional coaching practices for effective work with clients is to listen, and to listen well. As Jim Knight explains, when you listen effectively you "do not paint the words of others with your biases; you simply focus on understanding fully what the other person says." Listening is an active process that takes intentionality and focus. We must listen without bias and judgment, listen truly to understand only, listen for specific details that guide us to a deeper understanding of our client, and listen to move practice. Listening is not easy, but is absolutely necessary. I am convinced that if everyone tried just a little harder to truly and authentically listen, then the nature of all our conversations and all our relationships would dramatically improve.

Active Listening

"To listen is to continually give up all expectation and to give our attention completely and freshly to what is before us, not really knowing what we will hear or what that will mean. In the practice of our days, to listen is to lean in softly, with a willingness to be changed by what we hear." - Mark Nepo

Be authentic and intentional in your listening. Seek to understand. One powerful component of active listening is providing the client with the space to think aloud, talk through, and process their thoughts. How many times have you brought an issue to a colleague, only to realize that in the process of explaining the issue, you were able to come up with a solution, without the colleague even saying a single word? As a coach, we must provide the space and the environment for our clients to speak, to process, to discuss. Listening means that we don't interrupt, or try to finish their sentences, or step on the toes of their last statement. We provide space, pauses, and silence as they speak and learn and process.

Active listening also requires us to avoid the 4 patterns of unproductive listening as outlined in *Results Coaching*.

1. *Judgment and Criticism* - Listening with bias, judgment, and a critical ear of everything that is going wrong.
2. *Autobiographical* - Listening only for connections to your own life, so you can jump in and steal the show, sharing how what they are saying connects to you.
3. *Inquisitive* - Listening with off topic curiosity, going down a rabbit trail of random thoughts only scarcely related to what is being shared.
4. *Solution* - Listening for solutions and answers that will solve their problems.

As active listeners we intentionally focus on letting the above thoughts leave our mind as soon as they enter. We push all judgment, criticism, personal stories, off topic questions, and solutions out of our mind and stay focused on the speaker. We listen for the sake of the speaker, not for our own.

Celeste Headlee explains this concept in her TED Talk, "10 Ways to have a better conversation." She discusses the power of listening, letting go of the thoughts that enter your mind during a conversation, staying focused, not equating your experience with theirs, and more. If you have a few minutes, I strongly recommended you watch her presentation.

As Stephen Covey says, "Most people do not listen with the intent to understand; they listen with the intent to reply." Don't be most people. Be an effective coach and an active listener.

Listening Fors

As an instructional coach, we are required to listen for more than just understanding. We must *listen for* nuggets that we can use in guiding reflection, and moving the practice of our clients. Kathryn Kee, et al. in *Results Coaching* discusses the 5 elements we should be listening for in our coaching conversations.

1. *What the person wants:* Listen to hear the bottom line, the heart of the conversation. Beneath the details, listen for what it is the person really wants. A strong coach will be able to sift through the minutia to uncover the depth of the speaker's desires.

2. *Emotion*: Listen for emotions that are coming out in the conversation, and then call out those emotions. For example, "You are frustrated at the amount of time it is taking to complete your unit," or "You are excited to be on this new journey." Emotions play a strong role in our work and our lives, so effective coaches must know how to listen for these emotions and draw on them to move the conversation.

3. *Passion*: As you listen, determine what is truly important to the client, their deep passion, and their values.

4. *Options, possibilities, potential*: Listen for snippets in the conversation that show options, possibilities, and potential for the client and their work. Listen between the lines and to the nuances to pick up on these elements.

5. *What is already working:* Many times our clients will focus on the negative, or what they want changed, and discount the positives that are already occurring. As they share, focus in on what is going well, the positives, and what's already working, and then share these with the client.

Mastering this art of *listening for* will take your conversations to a deeper level. It will allow you to get past the surface level, the details, the nitty-gritty, and get into the heart and depth of the situation in front of you.

REFLECT
- ❖ What are your biggest challenges in listening and how can you overcome them?
- ❖ Think about a time when you felt truly listened to. What happened? What did the listener do? How did that make you feel?
- ❖ Review the *Listening Fors*. Which one do you want to focus on in your next conversation?

FROM THE FIELD

It's amazing what you can learn if you just listen. I mean, really. Stop talking, and listen to what is being said. I had an eye-opening moment when I first learned about the four types of unproductive listening. I realized that I commit autobiographical listening too much. And when I reflect even more, I realize that I can't stand it when people do that to me. I mean, I'll be telling a story to one of my colleagues about how a student of mine painted me a beautiful canvas of a sunflower... and the next thing I know I've been interrupted to be told about that one time their student bought them a car. It's selfish really, to constantly bring the conversation back to you, and I had done that so many times before. Ugh! I think we learned somewhere, at some point, that it's a good conversational skill to talk about yourself. And while I think that drawing connections from the speaker's life to your own can be a good thing, it cannot be all the time. Everything in moderation, right? We have to be able to decipher if our story is actually going to help the speaker at all, or if it's just going to turn the spotlight on ourselves. Once I stopped listening with the desire to respond with a story of my own, I was freed up to truly focus on the person and what they are experiencing. Sometimes stories will come into my mind while I'm listening, but now I let them go. The stories come in, and I open the door to let them leave. I'm not perfect at this, but I try. And I know I've gotten much better, which allows me to stay focused on what really matters - my client.

SEVEN NORMS OF COLLABORATION

Coaching by nature is a form of collaboration. As the Blended Coaching Model (p. 17) states, we should move in and out of different coaching styles, from facilitative to consultative, and everything in between. We exist to support and provide professional development to our clients by working alongside them to build the space, environment, and opportunities for learning, growth, and discussion. Because of the collaborative nature of this work, we must understand and follow the seven norms of collaboration as laid out by Garmston and Wellman and the *Center for Adaptive Schools*. Refer to the Appendix for more information on The Seven Norms of Collaboration.

Pausing

Provide space for your client to process by pausing after they finish speaking. The reality is that the *wait time* research for students is applicable to adults as well, and we must be sure to provide that space and silence for our clients to process. Many times a client will end their sentence, but pick up again with more information and details if given the time to process in silence. It only take a few seconds of space to make an impact.

Paraphrasing

To ensure strong listening, to validate our clients, and to begin to guide the conversation, coaches must become skilled in paraphrasing. Paraphrasing for a coach falls into three general categories:

1. Acknowledge/Clarify: This is the most popular form of paraphrasing, where we ensure we heard clearly what the other person is saying.

2. Summarize/Organize: This form of paraphrasing requires more intentionality to be able to summarize a client's statements and organize their thoughts into categories that will be beneficial in moving the conversation.

3. Shift Focus: This final form of paraphrasing moves the focus of the conversation to either get the client out of the unnecessary details and focused on the bigger picture, or to dial the client into a detailed focus and out of the visioning lens.

Paraphrasing Skill	Teacher Comment	Coach Paraphrase
Acknowledge/Clarify	"All we seem to do is practice for the state test and district benchmarking and I never have time to teach."	"You are obviously concerned about the students' real learning if all we are doing is assessing objectives for the state test."
Summarize/Organize	"You want us to meet with our team and differentiate instruction for a half-dozen different kinds of kids. I never have any time to just plan for the majority of the kids in my class."	"So there are two real areas of concern for you: planning for the majority of your kids and meeting with your team to plan differentiation."

Shift Focus	"I have some high kids, some low kids, and a whole bunch in the middle. Some of them will do well, some won't, and some will fall in between. That's just the way real life is."	"So you have a model for teaching and learning that's really like a bell curve - only a few can do really well and few must fail."

From *Leadership Coaching for Educators*

Posing Questions

An important indicator of a coach's level of effectiveness lies in his questioning abilities. We must be purposeful in our questioning, using the questions not for our own benefit, but for the benefit of guiding our clients' thinking and facilitating the space for them to reflect and pursue their own answers.

Questions should be open-ended, with positive intent, and authentic. Powerful questions "help move the teacher's thinking to a deeper and clearer level so that intentional action is set in motion" (*Results Coaching*).

> "It's not the answer that enlightens, but the question."
> -Eugene Ionesco-

Putting Ideas on the Table

As collaborative coaches, we provide more than just a listening ear. This means, that sometimes we will enter into a consultative coaching role, where we provide ideas, advice, and input to the client. The most effective way to provide advice and put ideas on the table in a coaching relationship is to simply ask the client for permission to share some thoughts based on what you've seen, read or experienced in the past. In this way, you continue to give choice to the client, and you ensure that you are presenting the ideas in a way that keeps the client in the driver's seat. Provide advice sparingly. Our role is to build capacity in our clients, let them do most of the talking, and work with them to come up with their own ideas, which cannot be done effectively if we simply tell them what we think they should do.

Providing Data

As Garmston and Wellman state in *The Adaptive School*, "Data have no meaning on their own. Meaning is a result of human interactions with data." The coaching relationship is where we provide the interaction with data for our clients.

Using the third point of data in a coaching conversation is the most effective way to guide a conversation. It maintains the relationship, takes opinion and subjectivity out of the equation, and gives a common focus on which to base our discussions. Use data often. The Work-Plan that is initiated in the beginning of the coach relationship requires the coach and teacher to build in evidence and data collection as they work on their goals. The Final Review then takes that data into account. Refer to the Appendix for the work-plan and final review documents. Also, refer to the Appendix for additional Data Collection tools and protocols.

Paying Attention to Self and Others

A coach's body language, tone of voice, appearance, and other nonverbal cues are important and necessary when starting a coach relationship, building rapport, and maintaining trust. Coaches, at all times, must be aware of how they are being perceived, regardless of intention. It's also necessary to pay attention to the needs of others, as outlined in the SCARF model by David Rock. Refer to Andragogy for more information.

Presuming Positive Intentions

One key component and secret ingredient of every coaching relationship is presuming positive intent. In paraphrasing, questioning, observations, feedback, in every element of coaching, we must always presume the positive in our clients. Presuming positive intent comes in the questions asked and the statements made. What we say can carry connotations that extend beyond the simple definitions of the terms. We must be intentional that the connotations in our statements and questions are always positive. Refer to the chart below for examples of positive presuppositions:

Comment	Presumption or Overt Message	Positive Presupposition
"Do you use technology in the classroom?	The teacher is not using technology.	"What technology applications are your students enjoying the most?" *Notice how this question assumes that the teacher is already using technology.*
"Do you know any discipline strategies?"	Your class looks like you don't know any discipline strategies.	"What discipline strategies are having the best impact on your students?" *This question is asked in a way that assumes the teacher is intentionally using discipline strategies and has already analyzed their effectiveness.*
"Have you thought about…"	You have not thought about it.	"What options are you considering? *This question positively presumes the teacher has already considered options for addressing the issue at hand.*

Adapted from *Results Coaching*

REFLECT

* Which norms do you think would be most beneficial to implement tomorrow in your coaching conversations?
* How can these norms improve your work as an instructional coach?

FROM THE FIELD

My favorite of these norms is presuming positive intent. I cannot emphasize enough how much of a difference this makes! Educators are smart people, and they can pick up on the between-the-lines of your questions. I very distinctly remember one time when I asked one of my clients a question that did not presume positive intent. In that moment, my client shut down and I visibly saw in his face that his walls were up. I knew I wouldn't get anything else done in that meeting, and it took a few additional meetings to bounce back from that. Presuming positive intent not only impacts myself and my clients, but other colleagues as well. Recently, in a PD planning meeting, one of the site administrators with whom I work made a statement that presumed positive intent. She turned to me with a smile on her face and said, "Did you catch that? I was assuming the positive! Wow, look at me go!" Even though positive intent was a focus only in our coaching program, it ended up in other areas as well. Another realization I had after presuming positive intent is that when my statements and questions presumed the positive, my thoughts did too. I noticed a difference in how I thought about a variety of things within my job, all of which were more positive. It is such an uplifting experience, and we can all use a little more positivity in our lives!

REFLECTIVE FEEDBACK

Reflective feedback consists of three components. The first is clarifying questions that allow both the coach and client to understand the issues and get on the same page. The second is a statement from the coach that picks out the strengths, the positives, and the values that are apparent in the client's comments. Finally, the coach asks questions that guide the client to either reflect on the past or look forward to future possibilities. Each type is outlined below and has been adapted from David Perkins' *King Arthur's Round Table: How Collaborative Conversations Create Smart Organizations*. Refer to the Appendix for a One-Pager of this information.

Clarifying Questions
- ✓ Clarifies an idea or behavior under consideration to ensure both coach and coachee are talking about the same thing

- ✓ Purpose is for understanding

- ✓ Examples: "How did your students respond to the process?" "Which resources most supported your ...?" "What data from ... supported moving forward?" "How do you see this program different from...?"

Value Statements
- ✓ Feedback statements that identify value or potential

- ✓ Communicates positive features toward preserving and building upon them

- ✓ Examples: "This could offer value to students with..." "The strength of the idea is..." "The scaffolding of your design will help teachers understand..." "There is evidence of thoughtful planning and preparation in..."

Reflective Questions or Possibilities
- ✓ Feedback to mediate thinking through the use of reflective questions and possibilities

- ✓ Communicates concerns and considerations toward improvement

- ✓ Examples: "What goals have your students set for individual mastery?" "What might happen if the students...?" "What learning gaps did you notice in student understanding?" "What other consideration are you thinking about with...?" "What connections have you made to..."

ANDRAGOGY

Adult learners have very specific needs that must be met for effective and powerful learning and change to take place. Dr. David Rock explains these needs in his essay titled, "SCARF: a brain-based model for collaborating with and influencing others," first published in the 2008 NeuroLeadership Journal. In this essay he explains the 5 components that must be in place for adult learning.

- Status
- Certainty
- Autonomy
- Relatedness
- Fairness

"*Status* is about relative importance to others. *Certainty* concerns being able to predict the future. *Autonomy* provides a sense of control over events. *Relatedness* is a sense of safety with others, of friend rather than foe. And *fairness* is a perception of fair exchanges between people" (Rock, 2008).

I encourage you to take the time to read the full article from the NeuroLeadership Journal.

You may also find it powerful to take the SCARF Self-Assessment to determine how each of these social drivers rank in your own life (www.scarfsolutions.com/selfassessment.aspx). Consider taking your clients through the SCARF Self-Assessment as well. You can then learn what is most important to them, and they can learn what drives you, as you both work together in a coaching cycle.

Additional adult learning principles that must inform our work as coaches are outlined below. These come from Jennifer Abrams' adaptation of the work of Linda Lambert, professor in the Department of Educational Leadership at California State University, Hayward. Each of the principles below align with the SCARF model and neuroscience research on adult learning.

- Adults have a drive toward competence, which is linked to self-image and efficacy.

- Learning is enhanced when adults are active, involved and self-directed.

- What is to be learned must hold meaning; it must connect with current understandings, knowledge, experience and purpose.

- We don't learn from our experience as much as from processing our experience – both successes and failures. Self-reflection, self-assessment, and self-direction are critical to learning and development.

- Learning is both an opportunity and a risk; it requires dissonance and change.

- Learning is the continual process of identity formation, or growing into more of who we are becoming.

REFLECT

- ❖ After reviewing the SCARF model, which drivers do you see most impact your work?
- ❖ How can you address the adult learning principles in your next coach meeting?
- ❖ As you think about adult learning needs, what tangible action steps can you do tomorrow to begin to increase the learning of your clients?

One of the teachers I coach did not take to me when I first started. In our district, all teachers are required to participate in coaching as part of their professional development. It's not an opt-in model. Because of this, I found myself working with teachers who did not want to work with me. But, this one teacher in particular was especially challenging. He would ignore me in the halls, give me short responses, and not do any of the things we talked about in our meetings. So, I took to the SCARF model to figure out how to meet the social drivers of this teacher. I realized that because I was younger than he was and because I was in a new position to the district of which he was unfamiliar, he may have felt that his status was being threatened. So, in my meetings to follow, I authentically pointed out the value in his expertise and asked questions in an effort to learn from him. For certainty, I made sure to lay out all of the expectations for coaching, showing the data and research behind the coaching model, re-introducing him to the forms and logs I would complete, and mapping out all of our future meeting dates. The autonomy was a tricky piece because all teachers were required to work with me, which took away choice from the get go. I did give him choice in his goal-setting, but since he didn't really want to work with me anyway, it didn't make much of a different. Addressing the autonomy driver came at a systemic level. I discussed with the site leaders the option of restructuring the coaching program to provide more choice to the teachers. We then worked to create a coaching system that outlines coaching tasks to complete, options of which cycle to participate in, and which topics to focus on. We also brought in a few more options for coaches, including our PBIS coordinator, and the site leaders, so if a teacher really didn't want to work with me, they had the choice to work with someone else. In relatedness, I found a common ground with this teacher through a hobby we both enjoy. Finally, in fairness, the more time I spent in coaching at that school site, the more he realized that this is a systemic initiative for all teachers, and that he was not being picked out of the crowd in any way. It's safe to say that by the end of that year, we worked wonderfully together and our professional relationship grew to the point of making positive change in the classroom.

THE WORK OF AN INSTRUCTIONAL COACH

COACHING CYCLE

Instructional coaching revolves around a coaching cycle, which can be utilized with either an individual client or a PLC/Collaborative Team. The steps of the coaching cycle are outlined below:

Initial Meeting: Goal Setting

The first meeting with a new client holds three purposes:
1. Getting to know each other
2. Setting the foundations and expectations for the coaching relationship
3. Establishing goals

Refer to It's All About Relationships (p. 20) to learn more about building trust with a new client. You can also use the Questions for a New Client resource found in the Appendix. Intentionality as a coach regarding the relationship building process is a necessity for a successful coaching cycle. One powerful way to build relationships in this initial meeting is by using the defining moments protocol, where each member of the relationship, both coach and client, share their five defining moments that led them to where they are today in their career. This opens authentic and genuine conversation, while creating deep opportunity for connection.

Also, in this meeting you will want to establish your ground rules and norms for the coaching relationship. These should be collectively determined with you and your client and should include discussions on: confidentiality, time commitments, the coaching cycle, expectations of the client and the coach, and any other topics important to you, your client, and your work together.

The final component of the initial meeting is goal setting. Goal setting is the driver of everything you do with your clients. Determine the goal you will focus on with your client, then clearly outline the indicators of progress, the steps to complete the goal, who is responsible, and a timeline. The Initial Meeting document found in the Appendix provides you with the structure and the questions to ask during this meeting as well as an outline for setting effective goals and collecting data on them.

FROM THE FIELD

I learned through the initial meeting and goal-setting process that some teachers are not used to the idea of setting goals. Sometime, they are so weighed down with the day-to-day they don't necessarily have the ability to look ahead, long-term, and determine where they want to be and what goals they want to accomplish. In fact, in one of my meetings with a client, I asked him what his goals were for our summer session, and what he wanted to accomplish by the end of the summer before the start of the next school year. He sat in silence for a while. Then he looked at me and said, "I don't know. To be honest, I don't often set goals because so much of my time and energy goes into running my classroom, grading papers, or putting out fires. I'm so used to being reactive, that I don't know how to look ahead." Wow! And I know he's not alone in this feeling. I realized that as I continue to work in support of teachers, I may need to take time supporting them in how to set goals for their classroom and their practice, and not just on how to meet those goals.

Demo Lesson

1. Design the Lesson (Coach with Client)
2. Demo the Lesson (Coach teaches; Client observes)
3. Debrief the lesson (Coach and Client)

Once the goal is determined, the remaining meetings exist to follow through on that goal using a gradual release model. Sometimes, this will require a demo lesson or model lesson that the coach does in the classroom, with the teacher observing from the back. This fulfills the first step of gradual release; the *I DO* portion. Teachers can use the Demo Lesson Observation handout found in the Appendix to record notes during the demo lesson. It is important that the planning of the demo lesson occurs collaboratively, so the teacher can see the effort that goes into the backside of the lesson, and can advise the coach on any pertinent information regarding students, etc. After the demo lesson occurs, the coach and client have a debrief meeting to discuss the lesson itself, observations from the teacher, ways to incorporate components of the lesson into the teacher's practice, and most importantly, evidence and data of student learning from the lesson.

FROM THE FIELD

Many instructional coaches are worried about the demo lesson. But, you don't need to be. I know I was when I entered my first classroom to demo that first year of coaching. I was worried that since I didn't have a rapport with the kids, they would act out on me, or that I would mess up in general. The reality was, however, that there was really nothing to worry about. I know how to teach, and I LOVE teaching. I planned the lesson with my client so I knew exactly what the students already knew and where they were going. When the time came to demo, it was like a little slice of heaven. Every educator who moves into a position outside of the classroom misses the classroom. The demo lesson is the chance to be back in that beautiful place. Plus, you get to showcase a strong strategy or new learning to the teacher and talk about how it worked with the students! It doesn't get much better than that!

Co-Teach Lesson

- Design the Lesson (Client with Coach)
- Co-Teach the Lesson (Client and Coach teach together)
- Debrief the lesson (Coach and Client)

The co-teach is the next step in the gradual release process for the client. It is the *WE DO* portion. In this step, the coach and client work together designing a lesson. Then they determine who will take which parts of the lesson, and they teach the lesson together. The coach provides enough scaffolding to support the client, while the client gets their toes wet and practices the new learning with the safety of the coach to back them up as needed. Afterwards, both the coach and client debrief the lesson discussing the lesson itself, observations they both made, evidence and data of student learning, and even more ways of incorporating it into the client's classroom. Refer to the Co-Teach Debrief form in the Appendix for guidance on the debrief conversation.

FROM THE FIELD

What I've discovered through my experience as an instructional coach is that the co-teaching lesson really doesn't require much from me past the planning stage. The teacher and I would plan a co-teach lesson and divvy up the components each of us would teach in that lesson. At the end of every co-teach planning session, I would explain that if, in the moment of teaching, the teacher feels comfortable to take any of the components from me and try it themselves, they are more than welcome to do so. I let them know that I would follow their lead and fill in as needed in support during the lesson. And you know what happened? Almost every single time, the teacher would end up teaching the entire lesson. I found this odd since they clearly explained to me that they wanted to co-teach. But, in the moment of co-teaching, I really wasn't needed. What I discovered was that my clients didn't need me to teach, they just needed me in the front of the classroom with them as a safety net and support. The majority of the time, I didn't do anything past introducing myself to the class. My clients knew that they could take the reins of the lesson if they wanted, and that happened, more times than not. Apparently, just having me stand there in support was enough for the teacher to feel comfortable in trying out the new learning.

Observation with Feedback

- Design the Lesson (Client, with as-needed support from Coach)
- Teach the Lesson (Client, with observation by the Coach)
- Debrief the lesson (Coach and Client)

Continuing with the gradual release model, the final step is the *YOU DO* portion. In this step, the client plans and teaches the lesson, while the coach observes, taking notes that will validate strong practices and provide reflective feedback for continued work in certain areas. They then hold a debrief meeting together to discuss the lesson, the observation notes, data and evidence of student learning, and next steps for the teacher.

In this step, the observation is the key component for moving practice. As the coach, a strong observation and feedback discussion can validate the teacher while providing guidance and support for continued improvement. On the other hand, an observation and feedback conversation that is unprepared or unskilled can leave the client feeling vulnerable, weak, and afraid of trying new things in the classroom. These observations are not to point out what is wrong or incorrect. Instead, these observations are meant as a way to use data and evidence from the lesson to provide reflective conversations that build capacity in the client.

The *Center for Educational Leadership* outlines a research-based, proven method of observing teachers and providing feedback that is pertinent, powerful, and effective. An adapted version of their Observation Form is included in the Appendix. According to *CEL*, observations should follow the outline below.

- Take notes in the left-hand column, writing down only what is seen or heard; evidence-based, non-judgmental, objective statements. If a teacher says something, write what is said, not what you think about what is said, or what you think about how it was said. The notes should be like a clerk's log in the courtroom...objective and factual only.
- In the right-hand column, either during or after the observation, write down your coding system (if you have one) as well as some feedback questions/statements. If you are observing for a specific element, this column is for you to connect the evidence from the left-hand column to the element or focus of the observation. If you have a question about something that was said or done, this column is where you would write that question.
- After you have finished your feedback column, hold a debrief discussion with the teacher. Ask them the questions from the feedback column, draw connections to the areas of focus, and use the evidence from the notes to guide the teacher's thinking.
- When asking questions ensure they are authentic. Do not ask a question you know the answer to, or a question that is really a statement in disguise. Be sure not to use questions as a way to manipulate the teacher into thinking what you want them to think. Instead, use this data to open their minds and allow for reflection on the strengths and areas of growth of the lesson. Guide them into their own solutions and decision making for future lessons. Do your best to stay out of the consultative model here.

- The feedback conversation should include:
  - Noticings (evidence from the observations)
  - Wonderings (what you are curious about based on the evidence)
  - Analysis (how the noticings and wonderings impact student learning and meet the area of focus and goals)
- Overall, remember to stay objective. Evidence speaks louder than opinions.

Refer to the Observation Form in the Appendix, which has been adapted from the *Center for Educational Leadership*.

FROM THE FIELD

My first observation as an instructional coach was terrible. I know this because on my coach survey form at the end of the first quarter, my teachers told me it was terrible. According to their ratings, my observations were not beneficial to their learning or growth, and they didn't find the feedback valuable. (Yes…there are pros and cons to making a survey anonymous!) So, I went to my supervisor and asked for help. I needed to get better at making my observations effective and I needed to do it fast. Thankfully, she let me participate in a training with the Center for Educational Leadership where I learned research-based, tried and true practices of observation and feedback. I've outlined a few of these practices above, and WOW did my observations and feedback change. When I received my teacher surveys at the end of the year, I was rated an average of 60% higher in the category of effective observations. Success!

Final Review

The final meeting of the coaching cycle is the final review. This is where the coach and client review the goals set in the beginning of the coaching cycle. Use the Final Review form in the Appendix to guide the discussion of this meeting. Document the strategic activities you participated in during the coaching cycle, the progress made toward the goal, evidence of the progress, and next steps to continue once the coaching cycle ends.

FROM THE FIELD

The final review meeting is my favorite meeting of the year! I get to sit down with the teacher and talk about all of the positives things we have accomplished in our work together. Sometimes when we are in the middle of the coaching cycle, we get caught up in the small things and lose sight of the big picture of what we are providing to our teachers. In the final review, we are able to step back and see the good work we have done. We are able to celebrate our successes and plan for the future. Believe me, if you follow this coaching cycle all the way through, you will feel like you can conquer the world after your final review meeting!

Collaborative Coaching Logs

Tracking the conversations and the work of the coaching cycle is an important step to staying focused on the goal, maximizing coaching time, and planning for the final review. It also comes in handy when analyzing data and proving the effectiveness of the instructional coaching program. Refer to Measuring the

<u>Impact of Coaching</u> (p. 51) for more information on coaching data. While we live in a digital world, the power of removing the barrier of technology in a coaching relationship is unparalleled. When a coach sits down to discuss goals, evoke openness and transparency, provide reflection and feedback, and ultimately work to build capacity and move practice, the best way is to be face to face, with nothing but a pen and paper between you. Opening a laptop in a coaching meeting takes away from the personal depth of the relationship, places a physical barrier between the coach and the client, and provides a source of distraction. Because of this, coaches are encouraged to take notes and track their work the "old school way", with pen and paper. Create a coaching binder which includes the work plan, the observation forms, the final review, and the collaborative coaching log. It personalizes the coaching, and maintains openness. Refer to the <u>Appendix</u> for samples of a <u>Collaborative Coaching Log</u>.

The Coaching Badge

Some districts are choosing to utilize a badging system for competency based PD. In a coaching program, this equates to a task list of what needs to be completed in order to successfully work through a coaching cycle. The <u>Coaching Badge Task List</u> includes the coaching cycle expectations, the documents and forms to be completed within the coaching cycle, a list of topics chosen by the administrators for the teachers to choose from for their focus area during their coaching, and a list of dates for the teachers to choose when their coaching cycle will take place. This badge is perfect for schools or districts who mandate that teachers work with a coach. However, it can be beneficial for the opt-in model as well, for teachers to know exactly what a coaching cycle is and to prepare for their work with their coach. Refer to the <u>Appendix</u> for a sample <u>Coaching Badge Task List</u>.

Putting it all together

A coaching binder puts all of these coaching documents in order of how they will be used in the coaching cycle. Copy these documents and place them in a binder in preparation for your first meeting with a client. The table of contents of a <u>Coaching Binder</u> are as follow:

1. <u>The Coaching Badge</u>
2. <u>Collaborative Coaching Log</u>
3. <u>Initial Meeting</u>
4. <u>Demo Observation</u>
5. <u>Co Teach Reflection</u>
6. <u>Observation</u>
7. <u>Final Review</u>
8. <u>Blank Notes Pages</u>

REFLECT

* How can you incorporate the processes and protocols of a coaching cycle into your work with teachers and teams?
* Which component of the coaching cycle are you most comfortable with, and which are you most concerned about? Talk to your supervisor for training opportunities on areas in which you'd like to grow.
* What are the benefits of following a coaching cycle like this?
* What are the benefits in using a coaching binder rather than a laptop in your meetings with clients?
* How can you adjust and adapt this coaching cycle and these forms to best meet the needs of your instructional coaching program?

COACHING CONVERSATIONS

"We face a crisis of communication. Although we may talk with dozens of people every day, we can go through entire weeks or longer never having a single, meaningful conversation." - Margaret Wheatley

"Better conversations can dramatically improve educator and student learning….Instructional coaches who learn to be better at listening, questioning, building emotional connections, and fostering dialogue become more effective. Communication is the lifeblood of coaching, and the more effectively coaches communicate, the more effectively everyone learns." - Jim Knight

> "Communication is the lifeblood of coaching, and the more effectively coaches communicate, the more effectively everyone learns."
> -Jim Knight-

Entering a coaching conversation requires preparation and intentionality. A variety of conversations ensue among a coach and client, and coaches need to be skilled in maneuvering through each type. Coaching conversations fall under the two categories of content and method.

The content is determined by the school site goals, initiatives, CSTPs, standards, frameworks, curriculum or other teacher specific choices, and includes topics like classroom management, curriculum, instruction, and assessment.

The method changes from meeting to meeting and is the means by which the content is addressed. It is valuable to explicitly discuss the method of the conversation as you begin your meeting with your client. For example, "Today we are in the planning stage of the coaching cycle, as we prep for the upcoming demo lesson. This means we will hold a planning conversation. How does this sound to you?" If a client has a pressing issue they need to address, then maintain flexibility with them, and ask them if they would like to move into a solution or problem-solving conversation instead. Drawing attention to the method of conversation at the beginning of the meeting allows you to maintain focus throughout the meeting and ensure productivity and effectiveness.

Results Coaching separates coaching conversations into the following four methods:
- Solution
- Goal-Setting
- Planning/Problem Solving
- Reflection

The Kansas Coaching Project, on the other hand, separates the types of interactions into 10 methods.

0	Did not see – Teacher may have been absent or an unforeseen event may have occurred (such as a tornado drill, school cancellation, assembly, etc.).
1	Enrollment Conversation – No implementation yet – dialogue about instructional practice or innovation is initiated by the coach.
2	Change Conversation – Focused dialogue about use of new practice or innovation initiated by teacher.
3	Implementation Conversation – Evidence of the new practice, curriculum, or technique

	being used; dialogue about its use occurs.
4	Preconference/Planning – A conversation in preparation for going into a classroom to conduct a model lesson or observe a teacher. An observation form may be co-constructed during this conversation.
5	Model Lesson – Done by the coach in the classroom on an agreed upon technique, practice, or content.
6	"Co-Taught" Lesson – This is usually a scaffold to the observed lesson.
7	Observation – Coach observes teacher conducting lesson on a coachable practice.
8	Feedback Conversation – Coach and teacher debrief the observation; teacher receives valuable feedback from coach on practice.
9	Strategic Integration – Lesson observed is highly developed – Ex: multiple techniques developed and infused with "real" content.
10	Refocusing/Adaptation – Teacher analyzing what students need and asking for it. This could be someone who tweaks the new practice or technique while maintaining the integrity of it.

Adapted from Susan K. Woodruff, Instructional Coaching Scale (2007)

These interactions closely follow the coaching cycle. Again the content of these conversations may be different for each teacher and school site, as you work through each of these methods.

Intentionality with the coaching conversation ensures that both the coach and client stay focused. Additionally, different protocols can be utilized depending on the type of coaching conversation that exists. The National School Reform Faculty website, *Power of Protocols* by Joseph McDonald et. al., and *Groups at Work* by Lipton and Wellman all provide protocols for the different conversation methods listed above.

REFLECT
❖ With what types of coaching conversations are you familiar, and in what types do you need more training?
❖ How can defining the coaching conversation before beginning a meeting enhance and improve the outcomes and productivity of that meeting?
❖ As you reflect on your own position, what content will you focus on in your conversations, and what methods will you use most often?

FROM THE FIELD

I meet with a colleague once every other week for peer coaching. It has been one of the best forms of professional development for me, and continues to be so. In one particular meeting of ours, I shared with her a challenge I was facing with one of my teachers who likes to complain for the sake of complaining. I would enter the conversation with this teacher prepared to plan the co-teach lesson, or debrief the demo, or set goals, etc., but before we could get to that work, the teacher would start complaining about this, that, or the other thing. So my colleague gave me some sound advice. She suggested that I provide space at the beginning of each coach meeting for the teacher to talk about what is on their mind. Then, afterward, we could enter into the meat of the coaching work. So, I decided to try this out. The next time I held a meeting with the teacher, I began the meeting by saying, "Our agreed upon focus for today, which was decided last meeting, was to plan our co-teach for next week. But first, is there anything you would like to discuss that has come up this past week? How would you feel about taking the first 10 minutes of this meeting to hold a reflection conversation on issues from the week? Then, after those 10 minutes, we can move into the planning conversation. What do you think?" The response was better than I could have imagined. By outlining the type of conversations we would start with, giving it a time limit, and then outlining the type of conversation we would end with, I was able to keep the teacher on track within the coaching cycle, while meeting his here-and-now needs from the week. Plus, when the 10 minutes was up, since we had both agreed to the 10 minute time-frame, we were able to put aside the complaining and move into the planning.

COACH MARKETING

Many districts follow the opt-in model of coaching, where teachers and teams are given choice of whether or not to use an instructional coach. In this model, it is imperative for instructional coaches to have effective marketing strategies that will reach into school sites and encourage teachers to utilize the coach.

The Challenges

As a coach begins her work on a school site, she will immediately be hit with challenges and roadblocks. Entering a school site with an understanding of the barriers affecting teachers today in regards to instructional coaching, will give the coach an upper hand in ultimately overcoming these barriers and recruiting teachers to her work.

Challenge	Description	How to address it
The *us versus them* mentality	Unfortunately, in many school sites, there is a divide between teachers and administrators, with ICs and TOSAs often feeling stuck in the middle. Many ICs are on teacher contracts, but since they are no longer in the classroom, and are sometimes housed at the district office, they are seen as administrators.	The best way to overcome this mentality is by addressing the negative tribalism and encouraging the staff that teachers and administrators are all on the same side of student learning. With the position of neither a teacher, nor an administrator, ICs and TOSAs are in the best place to begin to shift this divisive culture. When we talk with teachers one-on-one, we can encourage them into unity. Address it. Be explicit about it. Work to move through it.
Lack of knowledge	Teachers will need continual communication of what your position is as an instructional coach. Often times, sheer lack of knowledge is what causes teachers to put up a wall to ICs.	We must constantly remind teachers of our position, our role, and our expectations as coaches. We should explain clearly what our role is (refer to the Definition of Instructional Coaching p. 5 and Defining your Role p. 43) and explain clearly the standards for coaching (refer to the ICF Core Competencies in the Appendix). If teachers actually know what your role is, they will be more comfortable in opening up their classroom to you. It is important to share both the IC definition and ICF standards with the administrators as well. If an administrator is unclear of your role, then they will be less likely to encourage their staff to work with you.
It won't last	The nature of education requires constant change, growth, and movement to stay up to date on best	One way to address this is to share with the staff the Joyce and Showers Research (p. 6) on instructional coaching. Explain the

	practices, shifting technology, and updated standards. Because of this, many education programs come and go, which causes some teachers to experience initiative fatigue. They believe that coaching is just the newest fad in education that will disappear like "all the others."	effectiveness of coaching, why it exists, and how it can truly benefit them. The reality is, that even if coaching ended next year, the opportunity to work with a coach for any length of time improves practice and impacts student learning. Show them the data. The more informed teachers are on ICs and TOSAs, the more likely they will be to take part in it.
Fear of evaluation	A lack of understanding of coaching leads to teachers holding an unwarranted fear that coaching is actually a secret and manipulative form of evaluation.	This fear can be appeased through knowledge. Explaining what your job entails, the ICF Coaching Standards, the expectation of confidentiality, and the evidence behind your position should alleviate these fears. You can also take a coaching stance with the teacher and ask what they are afraid of, why they are afraid of it, and what they will need in order to address it.
Coaching is only for new or weak teachers	Once again, a lack of knowledge surrounding coaching leads many teachers to believe that it's only for brand new teachers going through an induction program, or for weak teachers that administrators are looking to release. Both of these statements are false.	With an understanding of a coach's role, standards, expectations, and impact, coaches can unwind this toxic thinking.

Defining Your Role to Teachers and Administrators

One of the most important components of marketing yourself in the beginning the school year is to define your role and explain what you do to teachers and administrators. Within your first week, you should seek to set up meetings with administrators and site leaders. In this meeting, discuss your role and the ways you can work with them to support them in their goals for their school sites, including training for the staff, PLC facilitation, and individual coaching cycles with teachers or teams.

Collective Definition
Another option at this first meeting of the year is to collectively define your role within the school and district. You can begin by providing the Instructional Coaching Definition (p. 5), showing the Coaching Roles (p. 12) and then working with the leaders on adjusting the definition and roles to meet the specific needs of the school and district.

Elevator Speech
Sometimes, however, you are not able to collectively define your role with a team of leaders, in which case, you can use the information from part one of this guide, What is Instructional Coaching (p. 4), combined with your job description to come up with an elevator speech about what you do. An elevator speech is a short, memorized speech that is just long enough to be shared in the amount of time it takes an elevator to

move from one floor to the next. This will come in handy as you run into teachers in the hall, or are asked in an informal conversation about your position. Below are some sample elevator speeches you can use, or adjust.

Elevator Speech Example (One-Floor)
"I collaborate with and support teachers in curriculum, instruction, and best practices by putting on trainings, facilitating team meetings, working with teachers one-on-one and completing other projects as needed. Ultimately, I seek to ensure teachers are given what they need to be successful in their classroom."

Elevator Speech Example (Three-Floors)
"My job is to collaborate with and support teachers as they work on new curriculum, initiatives or programs within their classroom, which I do by presenting staff trainings and workshops, facilitating PLC and team meetings, completing one-on-one coaching cycles, and a variety of other projects designed to support high levels of learning for all students. I love the opportunities I'm given to work with administrators on their professional development vision for their school, and to come alongside teachers as a colleague in support of increased student learning. Ultimately, I seek to ensure teachers are given what they need to be successful in their classroom."

Elevator Speech Example (Fifteen-Floors)
Okay, so this is not exactly an elevator speech, but it is a great introduction when presenting yourself to teachers at a staff meeting, or anywhere where you have time to explain in more depth what it is you do.

"The traditional form of PD is a one-and-done training, where an expert presents, while teachers try to grab one or two nuggets of information that they may or may not end up using in their classroom. There's no surprise that this model is ineffective. As a way to supplement this model and increase the effectiveness of professional development, more and more schools are moving to Instructional Coaching, which research proves is one of the most effective forms of professional development offered today. The ability to work one on one with a coach, focusing on a topic or goal designed specifically for you, your class, your students, and your curriculum is the most effective way to increase student learning. My job as a coach, therefore, is to come alongside you as a fellow teacher, to collaborate with you, model for you, co-teach with you, and support you in goals you want accomplished in your class. Research proves the power of collaboration in improving practice, just look at the PLC model! What I do, then, is provide that collaboration with you on a one-to-one level. I am a thought partner, another set of hands and brains in designing and implementing new strategies, and a resource to call on as you walk through the goals you've set out to accomplish."

As addressed in the challenges of Coach Marketing (p. 42) one of the biggest barriers to effective work is a lack of knowledge on the end of the teacher. The more we can explain what we do, the more change we will have in building rapport and impacting practice.

The First Staff Meeting

At the beginning of the year, you will want to work with site leaders to determine a time you can come out to the school site, speak to the staff, and introduce yourself and what you offer. At this initial staff meeting be sure to address the following:

- ➢ Explain your role and position. Use an Elevator Speech (p. 43) to get started.
    - ○ Be sure to discuss your position as a collaborating teacher. This is your opportunity to clear up the Misconceptions and Barriers (p. 42) on what you do and who you are.

- Review the ICF Coaching Standards with them, so they know what they can expect of you as a coach. Be sure to highlight the confidentiality component, and the focus on the client's perspective, style, and agenda.

➢ Discuss the data and evidence on the impact of instructional coaching.
- Use the Joyce and Showers Research (p. 6)
- Use your own data and evidence from previous years. Refer to Measuring the Impact of Coaching (p. 51) for ways to collect this data. Talk about what you accomplished last year, your effectiveness, and your impact on learning. Many teachers are weary of working with a coach because they don't really know what coaches do. So, show them what you do.

➢ Provide a teacher testimony from a teacher who has previously worked with you, if applicable. Include either a video clip or a direct quote from the teacher, or better yet, have the teacher present to share in person.

➢ Provide a digital or print copy of your Coaching Menu (p. 45) and explain what you can offer to them.

➢ Explain the Coaching Cycle (p. 34) so teachers know what they will expect when they work with you.

➢ End with a variety of ways they can get in contact with you, such as email, phone, or website, and an excitement to work with them throughout the next year.

The Coach Menu

Because instructional coaches take on a variety of roles, and because many teachers still do not fully understand what an IC does, a great strategy to market yourself to your teachers is to create a Coaching Menu. You can take the menu analogy as far as you'd like, but all it needs to entail is a list of the ways you can help support teachers. As you build your coaching menu, refer to the Roles of a Coach (p. 12) for more ideas.

Coaching menus typically include the following:
- ✓ Resource Provider
- ✓ Classroom Collaboration
- ✓ Demo Lessons
- ✓ Data Analysis
- ✓ Brainstorming Partner
- ✓ Co-Planning
- ✓ Technology Support
- ✓ Team Teaching Experience
- ✓ Intervention Support

*Refer to the Appendix for Coach Menu Samples

When advertising your menu, it's best to get it out in a variety of mediums:
- ➢ Print the menu and place it on the teacher bulletin board in the staff lounge
- ➢ Make copies of the menu and place one copy in each teacher's box
- ➢ Send a digital copy of the menu via email
- ➢ Present the menu to teachers at a staff meeting
- ➢ Present the menu to leadership at various administrative meetings
- ➢ Link the menu to your website

Make Yourself Visible

One of the most effective ways to market yourself as a coach and get into the classroom working with teachers is to make yourself visible. Coaching begins with relationship, so you must build that relationship. Here are some simple strategies to make yourself visible to teachers:

> ➤ Get out of your office and spend at least two days a week working in the teacher's lounge on school sites.
> ➤ Walk through the halls during breaks and at lunch, so the teachers see you on campus.
> ➤ Intentionally seek out informal contact with teachers, working on building a relationship with them first. This contact can come from hallway run-ins, meetings, lunch room encounters, etc.
> ➤ Eat lunch in the staff room with teachers.
> ➤ Meet with site leaders on a regular basis. Staying visible with leadership is just as important as staying visible with teachers. If leaders know you are available, you have a greater likelihood of getting into staff meetings and ultimately into the classroom.
> ➤ While on site, take the time to get to know everyone, from teachers to administrative assistants, to IT, and more. Think of it as campaigning for a vote.

Other Coach Marketing Strategies

Many of the coach marketing strategies have already been discussed in this section, but here are a few more to take your marketing to the next level.

> ➤ Set up a marketing plan right out of the gate. Put together a packet to present to leadership and staff with a description of what you offer, a coaching menu, a layout of the coaching cycle, valuable resources, and anything else you think will benefit the marketing campaign. Prepare for this before the school year begins so you can hit the ground running!

> ➤ Understand that it is All About Relationships (p. 20). If a coaching program is brand new to your district or school site, then be prepared for it to take at least a semester and sometimes even one full year of establishing rapport, building relationships, and explaining what you do before you are received with open arms.

> ➤ Create a website, blog, or other web-based site for teachers to access information regarding your work. Get this site into the hands of every teacher and administrator. Have your coaching menu easily accessible. Highlight a *Coaching Interaction of the Week*, where you focus on specific strategies that were implemented well, a new article or resource, or a Rock Star teacher.

> ➤ Send emails often to reach out and enlist teachers. After your initial presentation at the first staff meeting of the year, continue to send emails discussing the work you've been up to, and what you can offer to teachers. Attach your menu and other teacher testimonials to each email.

> ➤ Send out a weekly update or newsletter with resources, articles, research, a coming up section, dates to remember, and more. Learn how to start a digital newsletter by referring to this guide, created by Ryan O'Donnell, which can also found in the Appendix.

REFLECT

- ❖ What have been your biggest challenges in marketing so far? Which of these strategies will best help you in this area?
- ❖ Which marketing strategy stands out to you the most? Which one can you commit to doing this week?
- ❖ Make a marketing plan for the start of the year, mid-year, and end of the year enlistment of teachers. Share this plan with other coaches and your supervisor.

FROM THE FIELD

From my work supporting instructional coaches within the county, I've discovered the absolute need for marketing strategies. Our first two coaching PLC meetings revolved around this idea of how to get teachers to work with you and utilize your support as an IC. Since my work as an IC is in a program that mandates coaching for all teachers, I didn't run into this issue. However, every program that offered an opt-in model struggled with enlisting teachers. Through discussions at our coach meetings, and the sharing of resources online, we were able to put together a variety of marketing strategies, which I have outlined above. Coaches from almost every district within our county have used these strategies with strong results. My hope is that we have done the work for you, to allow you to start strong with your marketing plan and be able to focus your time and energy on impacting practice and increasing student learning.

PROFESSIONAL DEVELOPMENT

Part of the job description of an instructional coach is the planning, creation, and facilitation of professional development for teachers within the district. For many coaches new to the position, planning and presenting PD is an anxiety ridden experience. But it doesn't have to be.

> "He who dares to teach must never cease to learn."
> -John Cotton Dana-

A few key items to remember when planning PD is that you are a facilitator, not an expert consultant, which means your job is to create the space and environment for the participants to learn. Adults love choice and autonomy, they need to fully participate in their learning, and they need protocols to be most effective. Adults also need to know the relevance of what they're learning and how it applies directly to them in their classrooms. Make sure participants are able to leave with concrete strategies or resources to be used the very next day.

Before planning professional development take the time to outline a professional development plan with the site or district leader. The _Center for Educational Leadership_ provides a variety of resources to support leaders in preparing effective PD. This includes:

- Assessing the need by using the Determining the Need for Professional Development resource.
- Determining the most effective structure for the PD by using the Professional Development Structures Matrix.
- Analyzing the best modes of delivery for the PD in order to meet the expected outcomes by using the Professional Development Modes Matrix.
- Putting it all together in a Professional Development Plan.

Review each of these templates provided in the Appendix to successfully prepare for effective professional development.

Once you have a clear plan in place for the context, need, outcomes, and expectations of the PD, you can begin to actually design the content and delivery.

According to the Center for Educational Leadership, research about professional learning shows the following as the 7 most effective components of PD:

1. Choice
2. Ownership
3. Situated in teacher's own classroom and practice
4. Collaborative
5. Differentiated
6. On-going
7. Connected to system goals

Below are more strategies in effective adult learning through professional development.

Be a facilitator
When presenting PD, be sure to explain that you are a facilitator, not an expert consultant. Every member of an adult learning professional development session has their own experience, expertise, knowledge, and set of skills regarding the content of the training. It is important to frame the sessions as a space for all to learn from each other, which means, as the facilitator, your job is to create the structure and the space for

authentic learning to take place. Be sure to address the expertise and experience in the room and encourage collaboration and learning from each other throughout the training.

State your plan

Adults need to know where they are going and what to expect in a training. They also need to know why they are doing a certain protocol, activity, reading, etc. In the same way research shows the effectiveness of teachers explicitly stating objectives at the beginning of a lesson, we too must have objectives, an agenda, and a clear and direct plan for our participants. Adults crave certainty. They thrive when they know what is expected and what is to come.

Give Choice

Provide choice and options for participants. Do not force participation or call on a participant at random to share. Adults need to know that they are in control of their learning. They thrive with autonomy, so provide choice of where to sit, who to partner with, what to share, how to present their learning, etc. Consider differentiating certain activities or protocols based on level of knowledge. For example, those who are already familiar with the concept can work together on Reading A, and those who are brand new to the concept can work together on Reading B. Give them options!

Make Connections

Dr. Jim Knights talks in depth about the importance of making connections and relating with the participants in the room. Share stories of your own classroom experiences. Show them that you relate to them and connect to them on a personal level. Also provide opportunities for participants to relate to others in the training. You can do a *Stand-Up If* protocol where you call out a description and everyone who matches that description stands up. For example: "Stand up if you love the rain." "Stand up if you have been teaching for more than 10 years." "Stand up if you have a cat." Encourage participants to look around the room and make connections with others.

Use Protocols

Protocols are powerful. Dr. Tom Many shares about the importance of protocols in professional development from staff meetings to PLCs to trainings. Protocols ensure that every member of the group gets a chance to process and share. They systematize the learning so not one person is receiving the majority of the attention, but instead the learning is fairly distributed throughout all participants.

Keeping these elements in mind as you plan the structure, strategies, and activities of your training will ensure that it is effective.

The following resources and protocols are most beneficial for designing an effective professional development session:
- → *Groups at Work* by Laura Lipton and Bruce Wellman, published through Miravia
- → *The Power of Protocols* by Joseph McDonald et. al.
- → The *National School Reform Faculty* website under the "Free Resources – Protocols" tab, which can be found at www.nsrfharmony.org.

Each of these resources provides strategies, activities, and protocols a facilitator can use in a training to maximize participant learning.

For example, an effective 45-minute meeting would typically use three protocols:
- ➢ An activating strategy to pull the participants into the meeting, focus their attention, and engage them.

➢ A text processing strategy for participants to read, think, share, and process a piece of text that addresses the topic at hand.
➢ A summarizing strategy to pull the learning together and provide an opportunity for synthesis.

For longer trainings, add in a generating ideas strategy or an additional text processing strategy. Mix and match your protocols to best meet the needs of the content and the participants.

As you sit down with your topic for the training, think about the ways you can engage your audience and facilitate their learning. Keep in mind the 5 social drivers discussed in Andragogy (p. 31). Standing in the front and talking at the participants with a PowerPoint is not effective. Engage them and provide them opportunities to process their learning and apply their own knowledge and expertise to the subject.

REFLECT
❖ What type of professional development are you required to provide in your position?
❖ How can you build these elements into your PD?
❖ What protocols from the resources listed above stand out to you the most? Which one will you commit to use at your next PD session?

FROM THE FIELD

Professional development is perhaps my favorite part of being a coach. I love putting on trainings for educators! But, I am also not like most people because my comfort zone is on stage with a microphone. Nonetheless, PD is a large part of instructional coaching. I discovered that running a PD is very similar and yet very different to classroom teaching. When designing a PD, just like when designing a lesson, you have the content you want the participants to learn and the methods you will use for them to learn that content. We all have our go-to strategies in the classroom, and through the use of the protocol resources listed above, you will begin to create a repertoire of go-to strategies in a training. My favorite of those resources is Groups at Work *because it outlines, in a clear and simple format, the type of protocol, use, purpose, steps, and examples. In fact, most all of my trainings use strategies from that resource. For example, you can give participants a 2 page article and have them read it, then follow up with a 3As protocol where participants get in groups of 3 and each share something from the text they agree with, they want to argue, or they aspire to. As they discuss the article, participants bring their own experience and expertise to the conversation and make for a strong learning process for everyone. A very distinct difference, though, between classroom teaching and facilitating PD is the fact that you are working with adults with very specific social needs (the 5 drivers as explained above). Essentially, adults can do whatever they want and you can't do anything about it. You can't take a phone away from an adult for being on social media and ignoring everything that's happening in the training. You also can't use your go-to classroom management/ focus strategies to get participants involved because the participants are all teachers and they know all of those little tricks! However, I absolutely love facilitating trainings for educators because the depth of conversation is powerful, the learning is truly collaborative, and the networking and relationships formed are unbeatable. Once you figure out the methods, protocols, and strategies that work best, you will love every minute of the learning that takes place! Plus, when you make a group of educators laugh, you feel really good about yourself. I mean, let's be honest, getting 5th graders to laugh is one thing, getting adults to laugh is quite another!*

MEASURING THE IMPACT OF COACHING

As with every position in education, data and evidence drive our work. Coaches consistently seek to track their effectiveness in supporting teachers and increasing student learning. Along with the many ways coaching aligns with Statewide Initiatives (p. 8) and accountability, coaches can identify their impact on classroom instruction and teacher practice through surveys, feedback forms, coaching logs, goal-tracking data and more.

Determining Coach Effectiveness

Coach effectiveness and impact can be determined in a variety of ways. Listed below are a few of the most effective coach data collection practices.

✓ *Feedback forms and surveys*
  - These surveys should be completed by teachers after professional development sessions, PLC work, or individual coaching cycles.
  - Make sure the focus is on teacher growth and implementation within their classroom, as well as impact on student learning. It's also valuable to include a section about yourself as a coach, asking questions about listening, trust, observations, and more. Refer to the Appendix for sample Feedback Forms.

✓ *Coaching logs*
  - The coaching logs track the work of an instructional coach in teams or individual coach meetings. Depending on the log you use, you can also track your Coaching Interactions (p. 39), your goal-setting, and your strategic activities. Refer to the Appendix for sample Coaching Logs.

✓ *Goal tracking data*
  - This data outlines all of the instructional goals worked on with teams and individual teachers throughout the year. It measures the number of goals set, the amount of goals completed or met with significant progress, and the amount of goals not met. It includes the quantitative data, as well as qualitative, listing the goals, and explaining the progress. This data is most useful when showing alignment to school and district wide initiatives, and when working on the LCAP, and showing support for MTSS. Refer to the Appendix for Sample Goal Tracking Forms.

✓ *Coaching by grade, site, and topic*
  - Providing a breakdown of the amount of coaching completed within each grade level or department, and the amount of coaching completed within each site allows leaders to get a snapshot of the work you completed. Similarly, data on the coaching topics discussed from the year shows where the majority of teachers focused their professional development. This is mostly beneficial for site and district leaders who want an overview of the teams, sites, and topics of your coaching work. Refer to the Appendix for Sample Data collected in this way.

REFLECT

- ❖ Which of these methods of gathering data to track coach effectiveness do you think would best meet the needs of your program?
- ❖ What are some ways you can prove the impact of coaching in your program?
- ❖ Why is gathering data on coaching a valuable practice for your program?

FROM THE FIELD

I don't know about you, but I love getting feedback. I remember being in the classroom, pouring my heart into a unit, and being so excited to see how the students performed on the final assessment. I wanted to find out how I did as a teacher. In the same way, coaches need feedback. We need to know how effective we are and what we can improve. Reviewing the feedback forms and surveys from my teachers is one of my favorite things. I get to see how effective I was as a coach, pick out my strengths, and identify my areas for improvement. If you are asking the right questions, and making the survey anonymous, you will be amazed at the feedback you can get. I specifically remember some feedback I received after my first quarter of coaching. I sent out the feedback form to all the teachers I had worked with. When I got it returned to me, I was able to see how relevant my coaching was, how my teachers progressed toward their goals, and what their confidence level was in continuing the implementation after we stopped our work together. I was also able to see what I needed to improve. This gave me direction for my professional learning for the year! By the end of the year survey, I was able to I see growth in myself as a coach, and growth in my teachers through our work together.

The most effective form of data collection I've discovered to show coach effectiveness is the tracking of all the goals I worked on with my clients throughout the year, and the measuring of those goals as either completed, met with significant progress, met with some progress, or not met. I used evidence to support the placement of each goal into these categories. What is great about this type of data is that you can see the work that was completed, the evidence supporting that work, and the alignment of the goals with district and site initiatives. The cherry on top is that the data collected from both the feedback and the goal-tracking can be used by the district for evidence of effective coaching and accountability in the LCAP, etc. It's a win-win-win for everyone!

Coach Accountability and Assessment

As with every position, it's important to set goals, monitor progress toward those goals, and continue to grow, learn and improve. Coaching is no different. Listed below are some strategies for maintaining accountability with coaches, ensuring professional growth, and staying up-to-date and on track with your coaching program.

➢ *Regular check-in meetings*
- o   Hold consistent meetings between coaches and supervisors to review goals, previous work, progress made, and upcoming work. These meetings can range from once a week to once a month, but should not extend past every 4 weeks. It's important to stay updated on current coaching work in order to support coaches, site leaders, and teachers.

➢ *Shared calendars*
- o   A common form of coach accountability is in the shared calendar. Most coaches rely on their calendar for everything. In this case, the coach can share their calendar with a supervisor at the start of the year. This allows supervisors to see what the coach is doing, where they are working, and how they can best support their coach in the work they are completing.

➢ *Goal-setting*
- o   Similar to the CSTPs for teachers and the CPSELs for administrators, coaches have standards to work toward attaining as well. See Coaching Standards and Rubrics (p. 55), and decide on which standards would work best for your district's coaching program. Once these standards have been chosen, set up a meeting between the coach and supervisor to review the standards. The coach can then select 1-3 areas of focus throughout the year. Use the Coach Goal-Setting Form in the Appendix to select the goals, and track coach progress toward these goals both mid-year and end-of-year. These standards and goals can also be used in the evaluation process, similar to teachers selecting CSTP goals for their evaluations.

➢ *Evaluations*
- o   Some instructional coaches are on a teacher contract, which makes for an interesting situation when coaches are evaluated based on a classroom teacher evaluation form. Many programs are creating their own evaluation forms to use for instructional coaches, which must be approved by the teacher's union. If the instructional coaches in your district are not under a teacher's contract, then supervisors should work with Human Resources to create an evaluation specific to the coaching job. Use the Standards and Rubrics (p. 55) as a starting point for what to include on the evaluation form. You can also refer to a sample TOSA Evaluation Form found in the Appendix. In some instances, a manager evaluation may work for coaches. The important thing is that supervisors are giving coaches an opportunity to grow and learn through a formal evaluation.

➢ *Coaching digital log*
- o   Some sites extend their coach tracking beyond a shared calendar, and into a formalized coaching log, which is shared among coaches and administrators. In this case, all coach meetings are recorded in the log listing date, time, focus of conversation, type of interaction and next steps. Refer to Coaching Conversations (p. 39) for more information on what to track, and the Appendix for a Sample Log.

➢ *Weekly worksheets*
   ○ Another option for tracking coach work is through a weekly worksheet, which is shared with coaches and supervisors. This worksheet can include meetings from last week, professional development provided at school sites, coach professional learning, goals/projects for next week, and anything else you find beneficial. Refer to the Appendix for a sample Weekly Worksheet. Additionally, the weekly worksheet could include a reflection of the coach on their practice and their work in coaching. See the Weekly Reflection in the Appendix.

Coaching Standards and Rubrics

As coaching programs become more ingrained in our districts, we must provide the standards and support for continual improvement. Listed below are three sets of coaching standards that can be utilized within your program.

ICF Core Competencies

The International Coach Federation is the "leading global organization dedicated to advancing the coaching profession by setting high standards, providing independent certification and building a worldwide network of trained coaching professionals." These Core Competencies are used by coaches worldwide in a variety of careers from business to education to life. These standards are internationally recognized. Refer to a complete list of the ICF Core Competencies in the Appendix.

TEACHSCAPE Instructional Specialist Rubric

The Danielson Group and Teachscape has created a Rubric for Instructional Specialists that can be easily adapted to an instructional coaching program. See the Appendix for this Rubric.

Transformational Coaching Rubric

Elena Aguilar offers a transformational coaching rubric that is aligned with her book, *The Art of Coaching*. Many components from this rubric can be adapted and adjusted for your instructional coaching program. See the Appendix for an Adapted Rubric.

REFLECT

❖ What is the importance of providing standards for coaches within your coaching program?
❖ Of these three sets of standards, which one do you think will work best in your program?
❖ What are some other options for standards or rubrics to assess professional coaching skills?
❖ How can you use these standards in supporting coach growth?

FROM THE FIELD

I love having a set of standards for which to aspire. It's freeing for me to be able to access a document that lists the expectations of a good coach, in order to assess my abilities and see growth! My favorite set of standards is the ICF Core Competencies because they are internationally recognized and research-based in the field of professional coaching. Even though these standards are designed for all forms of professional coaching, not just educational coaching, I believe they are the best in terms of coaching expectations. Plus, I love that one entire category of the standards is on communicating effectively through active listening and asking questions. Those are tough skills to master!

On the other hand, one of the districts with whom I work has adopted the Danielson Teachscape standards for coaching in order to stay in alignment with their teacher expectations. Since their teachers use the Danielson framework, it made sense for their coaches to use the framework as well. That's the beauty of choice!

YOUR FIRST WEEKS AS AN INSTRUCTIONAL COACH

Starting a brand new position can lead to a lot of unknowns. Especially when it is a role that is still vaguely defined in many aspects. Here is a checklist of things you can do during your first few weeks as an instructional coach to prepare you for the journey ahead. All information on how to address each of these steps is included throughout this guide.

☐ Read this manual. Get to know instructional coaching.

☐ Meet with your supervisor to discuss specific expectations of your role. Each district varies in their purpose of hiring a coach. Be sure to discuss the roles of a coach and how much time is expected to be spent in each of those areas.

☐ Meet with other site and district leaders and administrators to discuss what you do and how you can support their goals in professional development and teacher capacity at their school site. Set up the first time you will come speak and present to the teachers at a staff meeting.

☐ Attend a Coaching Institute.

☐ Set up your calendar with color-coding and key terms for keeping track of your work. If done at the beginning of the year, with intentionality, your calendar can become your coaching log, your data tracker, and your entire coaching life. So create a system that makes sense to you. Color-code based on school site, professional development trainings, professional learnings, PLC work, etc.

☐ Review the ICF Core Competencies, or other standards your supervisor has chosen for your program, and set goals for yourself to track your own growth and progress in coaching throughout the year.

☐ Create a Coaching Menu.

☐ Put together a coaching packet to place in teacher's boxes or give to sites/teams that explains what you do and how you can support them. Include in the packet an easy to understand job description, a coaching menu, the ICF core competencies, or anything else you think would be of value in enlisting teachers.

☐ Put together a marketing plan for the start of the year, outlining what you will do and when, as you work to enlist teachers and administrators to utilize what you offer.

☐ Familiarize yourself with the coaching cycle documents and adjust them as needed based on your specific program and needs.

☐ Begin your own professional learning.

PROFESSIONAL LEARNING AND SUPPORT FOR COACHES

"As the [coaching] profession becomes more mainstream and established and as more and more school systems use coaching, it becomes increasingly important that educator-coaches have a deep understanding of coaching and have sufficient knowledge and skills to be successful in this role of change agent. Creating change in organizations is first about creating change in individuals. It's a delicate process...Credentialed professional coaches have high levels of training and skill in helping people and organizations change what they think, believe, and do, to achieve peak performance and boost results." - Karla Reiss *Leadership Coaching for Educators*

Training

Within Placer County, California
For upcoming training opportunities within Placer County and registration information, refer to www.PCOEedservices.org/Coaching.

- ➤ 3-Day Coaching Institute: Offered twice per year as an introduction to coaching, with time built in to practice and implement skills and strategies for effective coaching.

- ➤ Coach Network: A 3-hour professional development session and networking opportunity offered 3 times a year for coaches to continue improving in their coaching skills and strategies and to connect with others in their field.

- ➤ TOSA PLC: A 1.5-hour monthly professional learning community for Instructional Coaches (also referred to as TOSAs) to decide on a research-based strategy, go out into the field to implement the strategy, then return to discuss the impact and effectiveness of the strategy. This is a collaborative network for ICs to be a part of a team and improve in their work.

- ➤ Advanced Coaching Institute: A 2-day institute for coaches who have already attended the 3-day institute and are looking to deepen their coaching knowledge and skills.

Outside of Placer County, California
- ➤ The CUE (Computer Using Educators) Organization offers a TOSA specific conference known as the CUE ROCKSTAR TOSA EDITION. This is a conference designed specifically for Instructional Coaches in managing their various roles, implementing effective PD, and impacting teacher practice and student learning. Go to www.cue.org for information on their next TOSA camp.

- ➤ Jim Knight holds Instructional Coaching conferences, as does Elena Aguilar. Google search to find a training near you.

Other Professional Learning Opportunities

- ➤ Book Studies - Work through a coaching book with a fellow coach or administrator. Review the list of books below.

- ➤ Coaching Partners - Coaches benefit from coaching too. Find a fellow coach who would be willing to meet with you every 1-2 weeks to set goals, collaborate on upcoming projects, and coach you through planning, reflecting, problem-solving, or more. In turn, you would coach this colleague for them to receive support and for you to practice your coaching skills.

➢ Coaching Triads - If you have more than 3 coaches within your district, set up a time about once a month to run through a coaching triad. Coaching triads provide each member the opportunity to receive coaching on an issue, practice their coaching skills, and observe a coaching interaction. Refer to the Appendix for an outline of the Coaching Triad Protocol and an Observation Form to use in the triads.

Books and Resources
  ✓ *Amplify* - Thomas Many and Susan K. Sparks-Many
  ✓ *Instructional Coaching* - Jim Knight
  ✓ *Leadership Coaching for Educators* - Karla Reiss
  ✓ *Results Coaching* - Kathryn Kee et. al.
  ✓ *The Power of Protocols* - Joseph P. McDonald et. al.
  ✓ *Groups at Work* - Lipton and Wellman (Miravia)
  ✓ *Fierce Conversations* - Susan Scott
  ✓ *Having Hard Conversations* - Jennifer Abrams
  ✓ *Leverage* - Thomas Many and Susan K. Sparks-Many
  ✓ *The Multigenerational Workplace* - Jennifer Abrams
  ✓ *The Art of Coaching* - Elena Aguilar
  ✓ *Blended Coaching* - Gary Bloom et. al.
  ✓ *Better Conversations* - Jim Knight
  ✓ *High Reliability Schools* - Robert Marzano
  ✓ *The Marshall Memo* – Kim Marshall
  ✓ *Visible Learning for Teachers* - John Hattie
  ✓ *Common Formative Assessments* - Bailey and Jakicic
  ✓ *Coaching for Impact* – University of Florida
  ✓ *Learning by Doing* - Richard & Rebecca DuFour, Robert Eaker, Thomas Many

Blogs and websites
  ○ Center for Educational Leadership
  ○ Achieve the Core
  ○ Cult of Pedagogy
  ○ National School Reform Faculty
  ○ Instructional Coaching Group
  ○ Elena Aguilar Coaching Resources
  ○ Mshouser.com
  ○ PositiveEducator.com

REFLECT
  ❖ Of these resources, which three are you willing to commit to reading first?
  ❖ How can you protect your own professional learning time so you can continue to grow?
  ❖ What other book, blogs, websites, and resources can you add to this list to benefit you in your current role?

Who doesn't love learning? I'm pretty sure that's why I got into education, to never stop learning. That's also why I keep taking post-secondary courses for additional degrees and credentials. It's a sickness really. Thankfully, too, we have mandates in education that require us to continue learning as part of our job. We are so blessed! When I was a classroom teacher, my principal referred to me as the "Conference Queen" because I loved attending conferences. Did you say "Conference?" I'm so there!

What I've discovered through my position as an instructional coach is that professional learning is an even larger part of my job now than it was before. And this time around, my own professional learning comes with much more responsibility. As a teacher, I would attend conferences to learn new best practices that I could implement in my classroom, and maybe share to the staff at a staff meeting if my principal wanted me to. But now, when I attend trainings, and read books, and research online articles, I am doing it with the understanding that I must then impart this knowledge onto the teachers, coaches, and leaders within the county. I get trained, and learn, and grow, in order to train, and teach, and expand the knowledge of other educational leaders. What an empowering job!

I have to admit though, that sometimes it is hard to block out the time and devote it only to professional learning. It doesn't always feel productive in the moment. I realized that unless it's a conference, blocked out on my calendar, I find it hard to set aside the time. When I find new books I want to read, I end up reading them at home. Or when I get articles sent to me from my educational website subscriptions, I find myself filing them away to read later, until I have too many to read, that I can never catch up. The reality is, that the best way to combat this issue, is to start with one hour per week of time, blocked out on my calendar, and devoted only to professional learning. Once you can commit to that, up it to 2 hours per week. In the grand scheme of things, two hours out of a 40 hour work week is nothing compared to the power of learning and the change this new knowledge will make in your career!

HOW TO BEGIN AN INSTRUCTIONAL COACHING PROGRAM

So, you've seen the research and decided that a coaching program will meet your current district goals and support lasting change in your teachers. Now, the real work will begin. Listed below are the next steps to take in starting an instructional coaching program.

1. Decide on the outcomes of the program
   - Without a clear outcome or direction, your coaching program will lack the ability to maximize its impact.
   - What are you hoping to accomplish from this program?
   - What LCAP and MTSS priorities are being supported?
   - How did you identify this as a need?
   - What are your ultimate goals in incorporating an Instructional Coach into your district?
   - For information to assist in all of these questions, refer to Instructional Coaching Defined (pp. 5)

2. Decide on a job description
   - Refer to Roles of a Coach (p. 12) as you put together the job description. The Appendix has some Sample Job Descriptions to review as well.
   - Will your coach have administrative responsibilities? Will your coach be leading committees/teams, will your coach be focused more on individuals? Answer these questions as you determine the purpose of your IC.

3. Determine time allotments
   - Now that you have your job descriptions and roles clearly outlined, determine how much time you expect the coach to be working in each of those roles. For example: 50% in classrooms or with teams working through coaching cycles, 25% facilitating professional development, and 25% in other curriculum, instruction, or data based projects.

4. Work with the teacher's union
   - If your instructional coach is still under a teacher contract, set up a meeting with the teacher's union to develop a MOU including:
     - A definition of their role
     - Contract
     - Salary
     - Days worked per year. Understand that ICs and TOSAs need additional days, outside of the teacher contracted days for preparation, especially for beginning of the year PD.

5. Determine where to house them
   - Instructional coaches work primarily with teachers and would benefit greatly from a home location on a school site. Many districts house their coaches at the district office. While this may work logistically, it can send a message to the teachers that coaches are administrators, which is not accurate. Find a place for your coaches that will work best for all educators in your district.

6. Hiring the coach
   - Now that the job description, contract, and outcomes are determined, you are ready to find your instructional coach.
     - When you hold interviews, make sure you are asking the right questions that will show you the qualities of a Coaching Mindset (p. 20). Refer to the Appendix for Sample Interview Questions.
     - You may consider asking for evidence of effective teaching or running through a demonstration or scenario to determine their teaching and coaching competency.

7. Provide Training
   - Once you have hired the coach, provide them with training. Professional coaching is a skill that requires training and practice. It is more than just project completion, so be sure you support your coaches in learning how to transition from classroom teacher to instructional coach. Refer to Professional Learning (p. 57) for opportunities.

Another excellent source to use for information on starting an instructional program is _Coaching for Impact_ by Learning Forward.

COACHING
TIPS/TRICKS

TIPS AND TRICKS

Sometimes the most beneficial learning we can receive is tips and tricks straight from the experience of those currently in the position. Below are short and sweet snippets from over a dozen coaches, who have lived and breathed the work of coaching. Hopefully these will help you as you discover your own coaching craft.

Stay Connected

→ Use Twitter for staying connected with newest research and insights in education as you build your Professional Learning Network.

→ Make sure you take the time to get to know everybody on a school site. Build relationships and ensure that everyone is comfortable with your presence on campus.

→ Start your day at a school site, not at the office. Eat lunch in the staff rooms of the schools during their lunch hours. Make yourself visible.

→ Get face time with site principals on a regular basis for a quick 30 minute check-in meeting once or twice a month.

Use Technology

→ Utilize technology to make your job easier, for example iCal can pull in both Gmail and Outlook calendars.

→ Voxer is a great platform for quick and easy communication

→ Twitter will allow you to grow your PLN and connect with other ICs

→ Have a system with your email flow. Perhaps you don't open an email until you're ready to answer it, or you have files and folders to organize your email to-dos and responses.

→ Use shared Google Docs and other G-Suite options in your organization. Look into Team Drive for Google and task assignment.

→ Google Keep helps organize your notes and to-do lists

→ Utilize the bookmark bar in Google Chrome to have quick access to your most important online documents and websites.

→ Padlet or Symbaloo helps organize links, documents, and notes into an easy to access online location. Create a padlet for PD, one for Instructional Coaching, one for teachers, etc.

→ You Can Book Me is a booking program for teachers to log-in and schedule meetings with a coach.

Other Tips/Tricks

→ Have a physical notebook to take meeting notes, keep business cards, and more. Keep this notebook in chronological order for easy access to notes from past meetings.

→ Set-up quick access to bell schedules and prep periods for each school site you support. This will come in very handy.

→ Create a staffing list straight out of the gate. Know who is where and when.

The Almighty Calendar

→ Share your calendar with fellow ICs and TOSAs, supervisors, and administrators. This allows everyone to be on the same page.

→ Use your calendar for reminders and tasks.

→ When enlisting teachers and scheduling meetings, block out the tentative dates on your calendar as you wait for a response. If you send a specific date and time to a teacher, they may not respond for two days. If you haven't blocked out that time, you could easily schedule over it. Every time you propose a tentative meeting, hold it on your calendar.

→ When you schedule coach meetings and appointments, allow for 30 minutes after the meeting to finish any forms and documentation, and travel to your next site. Don't forget travel time.

→ Block off times to prep for coaching, PD, etc. If you do not enter the time into your calendar and mark it as busy, then the time will get scheduled over. Keep your planning time sacred.

→ When planning professional development build in time to plan and prep for the professional development, and then don't schedule over that time. When just starting out, a good rule of thumb is to give yourself at least *double the length of the training* for planning and prep. If you can, give yourself triple, until you get used to the flow and become quicker at planning.

→ Color-code your calendar to distinguish between classroom coaching, meetings with site leaders, professional development, projects, etc. Come up with a system at the beginning of the year and stick to that system. Once you learn it, it will be a life-saver for you. This color-coding can also be combined with key terms to make searching within your calendar an easy process. Your calendar will be where you track everything from coaching cycles to to-do lists to mileage if done correctly. Take the time to map out how you will code your calendar.

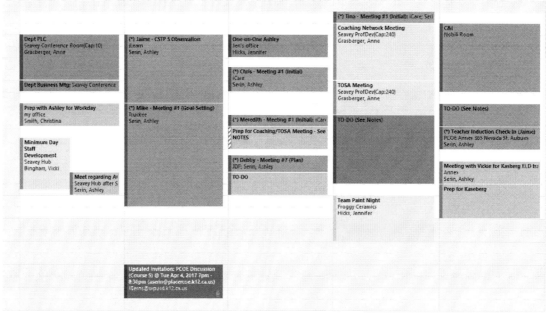

*Sample color coded calendar (eg: Blue is classroom coaching, yellow is professional development, green is prep for PD, etc.)

REAL TALK

Listed below are quotes directly from coaches in the field, to help those new to the profession. I have included, below each statement, additional thoughts in an effort to expand and elaborate.

"Take a deep breath and don't expect a lot at the beginning. It's not going to be instant to see changes and make adjustments like it was in the classroom. It's like walking in wet concrete. It won't change overnight. Be patient."
> ➤ Many coaches and TOSAs come straight out of the classroom, where if a lesson bombed, they could scrap it, and find a new one to implement before the end of the day. The decision was on the teacher, and could be implemented as soon as the teacher desired. In an instructional coaching position, however, it doesn't work that quickly. Be prepared for the slow process of implementation, meeting the needs of all stakeholders, and supporting in-depth, lasting change among your colleagues. It won't happen overnight, but the consistency and depth in which you build capacity in the teachers will ultimately impact student learning for the long haul.

"Find the balance between protecting your time and saying yes."
> ➤ Many times coaches and TOSAs who are new to the job and don't know exactly what they are expected to do will find themselves saying yes to every project, assignment, or task thrown their way. They are balancing the desire to be helpful and the time needed to do the powerful work of coaching. This is why it's so important to clearly define your role with your supervisor and to meet with your principals and site leaders at the beginning of the year to explain what it is you do. If you have this meeting at the beginning of the year, and an administrator asks you to do something not within the scope of your work, you can politely decline as you choose to focus on the responsibilities for which you have been hired. Coaches and TOSAs are not meant to take on the projects that administrators don't want to do. You are here for a purpose and must protect that purpose.

"I learned a lot about myself, what I'm good at, skills I didn't realize I had."
> ➤ This job is so different than classroom teaching and will stretch you out of your comfort zone and into areas you never thought you would go. Through this process you will discover so much about your abilities, skills, and leadership attributes. Enjoy this!

"I have a new appreciation for culture and how important the culture of a school is. In this position I get to learn about the different leadership styles and the different schools within the district."
> ➤ Most ICs do not land in a coaching position and decide to stay there forever. In fact, most ICs commit to the position for 3-5 years before heading into an administrative role. Some districts will only allow a person to be in a coaching position for 5 years before they are forced to move on, and some districts will only hire ICs who they see moving into an administrative role at some point in the future. Regardless of where you land in this process, the ability to work with all school sites and leadership styles provides you with insight into the type of leader you want to be and the school site in which you may someday want to work.

"Being able to go to the bathroom whenever you want is nice, but being able to eat whenever and wherever you want is not. Unfortunately, you don't have a home base for your lunches each day, so you tend to eat out more, which leads to a few extra pounds by the end of the year."
> ➤ One positive of leaving the strict bell schedule of the classroom is definitely the ability to use the restroom whenever you want! But the lunch situation is real. Traveling from school site to school site each day makes it very difficult to pack a lunch. Healthy eating goes out the window, as does all of your cash, so make a plan for bringing lunches and saving money while in a traveling role.

"If something isn't working, it's okay to stop using it and try something else. Be flexible. Try new things."
> In the same way you tried new strategies and techniques in the classroom, do the same in your position as a coach. Try out one organizational method, and if that doesn't work, try a different one. Be open and flexible until you get into your rhythm. It may take the whole year to finally feel comfortable, so be aware of that.

"I wish I had created a needs survey at the start of the year to send to teachers to find out what topics they are interested in, how they prefer to receive professional development, and what they want and need, before I jumped into planning trainings and PD for them."
> Determining needs right up front makes for an easier process in designing PD. It engages the teachers and increases relevance. Surveys are always informative, but be aware of sending out too many. Work with site leaders on when you can get this feedback and the best way to ensure a vast amount of responses.

"I wish I had known how difficult secondary teachers can be...or everyone actually...when it comes to soliciting my support and collaboration. I didn't know how to explain what exactly we do, and that we are really here to help. I learned to be so careful regarding the perception of TOSAs from other people, and trying to overcome the divisive *us versus them* mentality."
> This was a common issue among ICs and TOSAs their first year on the job. Refer to Coach Marketing (p. 42) to get ideas on how to combat this.

"I was surprised that administrators did not do more to take advantage of the coaches at their school sites. I wish I had some information to give to admin to show the importance of our positions and how we can impact the classroom."
> Many administrators are just like teachers in their lack of knowledge of how a coach can benefit them. Set up a meeting with the administrators at the start of the year to explain what you do and how you can support them in their PD goals. Provide them with a coach menu and packet as discussed in the coach marketing section. Remember, it's not that they don't want to utilize you, it's that they don't know exactly how they can utilize you.

"It will be one year of building relationships. It's important to establish at least one strong connection at each site, form trust, and describe what you do."
> I cannot overemphasize the importance of building relationships. Be prepared for your first semester and even your first year to be mostly relationship building. If you go into the job knowing the importance of this, you will most likely accomplish this goal even sooner.

BIBLIOGRAPHY

Aguilar, Elena. *The Art of Coaching: Effective Strategies for School Transformation*. San Francisco: Jossey-Bass, 2013. Print.

Aguilar, Elena. *Resources*. Elena Aguilar, 2016. Web. 16 June 2017. <http://elenaaguilar.com/resources>.

Aguilar, Elena. *Transformational Coaching Rubric*. San Francisco: Jossey-Bass, 2013. PDF. <http://elenaaguilar.com/wp-content/uploads/2016/04/transformational_coaching_rubric.pdf>.

Anderson, Karen Anderson, PCC M.Ed. "Listening - the Psychological Equivalent of Air." Results Coaching Global, 10 Mar. 2016. Web. 16 June 2017. <http://resultscoachingglobal.com/listening-is-the-psychological-equivalent-of-air/>.

Bloom, Gary, Claire Castagna, Ellen Moir, and Betsy Warren. *Blended Coaching: Skills and Strategies to Support Principal Development*. Moorabbin, Vic.: Hawker Brownlow Education, 2009. Print.

"California State PTA." *Eight Priorities Create Accountability*. The California State PTA, n.d. Web. 16 June 2017. <http://capta.org/focus-areas/lcfflcap/priority-areas/>.

Center for Educational Leadership | Articles, Resources, PD. University of Washington, n.d. Web. 16 June 2017. <https://www.k-12leadership.org/>.

"Coaching Roles." *Coaching Matters*. Learning Forward. <https://learningforward.org/docs/coachingmatters/killiontoolch5-4.pdf>.

Cooper, Dr. J. David. *Professional Development: An Effective Research-Based Model*. Houghton Mifflin Harcourt. <http://www.washingtonstem.org/STEM/media/Media/Resources/Professional-DeveloPment-An-Effective-Research-Based-Model-COOPER.pdf>.

Echeverria, R.O., and Olalla J. *Mastering the Art of Professional Coaching*. San Francisco: The Newfield Group, 1990. Print.

Fact Sheet: State Priorities for Funding: The Need for Local Control and Accountability Plans. Rep.: CSBA, August 2013. <https://www.csba.org/GovernanceAndPolicyResources/FairFunding/~/media/CSBA/Files/GovernanceResources/GovernanceBriefs/2013_08_LCFF_Fact_Sheet-funding_priority.ashx>.

Fink, Stephen L. *Leading for Instructional Improvement: How Successful Leaders Develop Teaching and Learning Expertise*. Hoboken, NJ: Jossey-Bass, 2011. Print.

Gladwell, Malcolm. *Outliers: The Story of Success*. New York: Back Bay , Little, Brown, 2008. Print.

Headlee, Celeste (2015, May). *10 Ways to Have Better Conversations* [Video File]. Retrieved from <https://www.ted.com/talks/celeste_headlee_10_ways_to_have_a_better_conversation>.

ICF: International Coaching Federation. Web. 16 June 2017. <https://www.coachfederation.org/>.

Isaacs, William, and Peter M. Senge. *Dialogue and the Art of Thinking Together: A Pioneering Approach to Communicating in Business and in Life*. New York: Doubleday, a Division of Random House, 2006. Print.

Kee, Kathryn, et. al. *RESULTS Coaching: The New Essential for School Leaders*. Thousand Oaks, CA: Corwin, 2010. Print.

Killion, Joellen, and Cindy Harrison. *Taking the Lead: New Roles for Teachers and School-based Coaches*. Oxford, OH.: National Staff Development Council, 2006. Print. Adapted.

King, Debi, et al. *Instructional Coaching: Professional Development Strategies That Improve Instruction*. Annenberg Institute for Education Reform. Providence, RI. <http://www.annenberginstitute.org/sites/default/files/product/270/files/InstructionalCoaching.pdf>.

Knight, Jim. *Better Conversations: Coaching Ourselves and Each Other to Be More Credible, Caring, and Connected*. Thousand Oaks, CA: Corwin, A Sage, 2016. Print.

Knight, Jim. *Instructional Coaching: A Partnership Approach to Improving Instruction*. Thousand Oaks, Calif: Corwin, 2009. Print.

Many, Thomas W., and Susan K. Sparks-Many. *Leverage: Using PLCs to Promote Lasting Improvement in Schools*. Thousand Oaks: Corwin, 2015. Print.

Many, Thomas W., et al. *Amplify your Impact: Coaching Collaborative Teams in PLCs at Work*. Bloomington: Solution Tree Press, 2018. Print.

MTSS Components: Multi-Tiered System of Supports. CA Dept of Education, 13 May 2016. Web. 16 June 2017. <http://www.cde.ca.gov/ci/cr/ri/mtsscomponents.asp>

Perkins, David. *King Arthur's Round Table: How Collaborative Conversations Create Smart Organizations*. Wiley, 01 Jan. 1970.

Reiss, Karla. *Leadership Coaching for Educators: Bringing out the Best in School Administrators*. Thousand Oaks, CA: Corwin, 2015. Print.

Rock, David. *"*SCARF: A Brain-based Model for Collaborating with and Influencing Others.*"* NeuroLeadership Journal, (2008). <https://neuroleadership.com/>.

Rubrics for Instructional Specialists. Teachscape: The Danielson Group. PDF. <https://www.danielsongroup.org/framework/>.

Schmoker, Michael J. *Results Now: How We Can Achieve Unprecedented Improvements in Teaching and Learning.* Heatherton, Vic.: Hawker Brownlow Education, 2007. Print.

Stone, D. Patton, B., and Heen, S. *Difficult conversations: How to discuss what matters most.* New York: Penguin.

The University of Florida Lastinger Center for Learning, Learning Forward, & Public Impact. (2016). *Coaching for impact: Six pillars to create coaching roles that achieve their potential to improve teaching and learning.* Gainesville: University of Florida Lastinger Center; Oxford, OH: Learning Forward; and Chapel Hill, NC: Public Impact. Retrieved from <www.learningforward.org/coaching-for-impact/>.

Woodruff, Susan K. "Instructional Coaching Scale: Measuring the Impact of Coaching Interactions." *Instructional Coaching Group* (2007). <http://effectiveeducationalcoaching.weebly.com/uploads/2/3/5/6/23564284/icg_woodruff_scale .pdf>.

APPENDIX

BY ORDER OF APPEARANCE

All resources can be found at www.PCOEedservices.org/coaching or in the PCOE Coaching Resources Google Folder at https://goo.gl/18yftb.

WHAT IS INSTRUCTIONAL COACHING? (PP. 1-17)

INSTRUCTIONAL COACHING PRINCIPLES (PP. 19-32)

THE WORK OF AN INSTRUCTIONAL COACH (PP. 33-61)

The Coaching Cycle (pp. 34-38)

Coach Marketing (pp. 42-47)

Professional Development (pp. 48-50)

All resources can be found at www.PCOEedservices.org/coaching or in the PCOE Coaching Resources Google Folder at https://goo.gl/18yftb.

COACHING LOGS...**https://goo.gl/MP1PvP**
Collaborative Coaching Log https://goo.gl/Jof9kb
Collaborative Coaching Log (Ver. 1) https://goo.gl/7xdpDh
Collaborative Coaching Log (Ver. 2) https://goo.gl/5sk2JG
Collaborative Coaching Log (Ver. 3) https://goo.gl/ULD8Gc
Digital Coaching Log https://goo.gl/NAeUT5

COACH MENU SAMPLES..**https://goo.gl/A1mxH6**
Coach Menu Sample #1 ....https://goo.gl/kv4KZx
Coach Menu Sample #2 ....https://goo.gl/MjwWp5
Coach Menu Sample #3 ....https://goo.gl/eQPFyj
Coach Menu Sample #4 ....https://goo.gl/KhUPD7
Coach Menu Sample #5 ....https://goo.gl/WbZ375

COACHING CONVERSATION TOOLS AND RESOURCES ....**https://goo.gl/kqLevc**
Coaching Conversation Analysis Tool https://goo.gl/e45tfG
Coaching Sentence Stems ....https://goo.gl/SsXZDg
Coaching Session Planning Tool ....https://goo.gl/khhFdu
Instructional Coaching Interactions ....https://goo.gl/DJzMtz
Reflective Feedback https://goo.gl/KouSp9
Questions for a New Client https://goo.gl/AN7zs2
Collaborative Coaching Log https://goo.gl/Jof9kb
Digital Coaching Log https://goo.gl/NAeUT5

THE COACH CYCLE FORMS (COACHING BINDER) **https://goo.gl/QudoS4**
Basic Coaching Badge https://goo.gl/RCt4Pe
Collaborative Coaching Log https://goo.gl/Jof9kb
Initial Coach Meeting https://goo.gl/f2h5h6
Demo Observation https://goo.gl/RMxRj4
Co-Teach Debrief https://goo.gl/cVLu83
Classroom Observation ....https://goo.gl/JBcJYh
Final Review https://goo.gl/6iAXyF
Blank Notes Pages ....https://goo.gl/AjPbtx

COACHING DATA, FEEDBACK FORMS, AND EVALUATIONS **https://goo.gl/THX7b5**
Coaching Data Sample ....https://goo.gl/mTBCNb
Coaching Feedback Form Sample ....https://goo.gl/TCMwtt
Instructional Coaching Data Template ....https://goo.gl/fcmYYt
Mid-Year Teacher Survey Sample https://goo.gl/Krz1UP
Professional Learning Survey Sample ....https://goo.gl/XkWBJB
Three Minute Feedback Form Sample https://goo.gl/1hgiYk
TOSA Evaluation Form Sample https://goo.gl/V89mst

Made in the USA
Columbia, SC
28 November 2018